SOCIO-ECONOMY OF INDIA

The First 50 Years and Beyond

SOCIO-ECONOMY OF INDIA

The First 50 Years and Beyond

Edited by
P. JEGADISH GANDHI
Professor of Economics,
Voorhees College, Vellore

and

Hony. Director,
Vellore Institute of Development Studies

DEEP & DEEP PUBLICATIONS
F-159, Rajouri Garden, New Delhi-110027

ISBN 81-7629-080-7

Typeset by ASHISH TECHNOGRAPHICS, 3190, Mohindra Park, Shakur Basti, Delhi-110034.

Printed in India at ELEGANT PRINTERS, A 38/2, Mayapuri, Phase I, New Delhi-110064

Published by DEEP & DEEP PUBLICATIONS, F-159, Rajouri Garden, New Delhi-110027. Phones : 5435369, 5440916

To

The Living Lord

whose

'Invisible Hand'

guides me

Contents

Preface

To memoralize the 50th year of our Independence (1947-1997) and the 80th year of Jubilation (1918-97) of the All India Economic Association, I ventured to bring out an edited volume entitled, *Socio-Economy of India: The First 50 Years and Beyond.* This is my second attempt, the earlier being *Economic Reforms: Mid-way Reflections, 1994,* (a publication of the IEA Trust for Research and Development)—to compile the valuable comments exclusively from some of the Conference Presidents of IEA. Apart from their professorial discourse and research, the past Presidents had the privilege of playing the role of national policy-makers in diverse fields in the post- Independence period. In this volume a band of economists have not only presented critical accounts of the achievements and aberrations in the 50 years of India's socio-economic development, but 'looked beyond' with a package of change-propellers for a better Indian society in the 21st Century.

I owe a deep sense of gratitude to all distinguished contributors—Dr. M.V. Mathur for his commitment to send a paper in despite of his physical discomfiture, Dr. P.R. Brahmananda for his constant go-go signal in all my academic sojourns, Dr. D.M. Nanjundappa for his thoughtful response, Dr. D.L. Narayana for his encouragement over phone, Dr. Alak Ghosh for his fine gestures and Dr. V.R. Panchamukhi for his valuable suggestions.

I remain thankful to the past Presidents of IEA—Dr. I.G. Patel, Former Governor of RBI, Prof. Amartya Sen, Harvard

University, Cambridge, USA, Dr. C. Rangarajan, Governor of RBI, Dr. Kamta Prasad, Chairman, Institute for Resource Management and Economic Development, Delhi, Prof. Ruddar Datt, Former Principal, School of Correspondence Courses and Continuing Education, University of Delhi and Prof. Kanta Ahuja, Senior Visiting Fellow, Institute of Development Studies, Jaipur—for their letters of appreciation.

The publication of this book would not have been possible—within a short span time—without the timely assistance of Prof. Debendra Kumar Das, University Department of Economics, B.R.A. Bihar University, Muzaffarpur and the willing cooperation of Mr. G.S. Bhatia, Deep & Deep Publications, New Delhi.

Vellore P. JEGADISH GANDHI

Acknowledgement

Thanks are due to the Editor, *The Hindu-Business Line* for the permission given to use the published articles of Dr. P.R. Brahmananda—"Role of Agricultural Development", "Declining Farm and Food Growth", and "A New Deal for Agriculture" and of Dr. V.R. Panchamukhi—"Indian Industry—The Next 50 Years".

Vellore P. JEGADISH GANDHI

Introduction

The Indian Freedom Movement and post-Independence development is a story of struggles, sacrifices, successes and surging realities. The year 1997 marks a period of 'looking back' achievements and appraisals of 50-years of India's socio-economic development and 'looking forward' to challenges in the 21st Century. From the shedding of Colonial shackles to ushering in a socialist pattern of society and now adopting a market-driven system, Indian economy has shown its inherent resilience and resistance in the transformation of society.

At the Golden Jubilee of Independence, Indian economy presents a mixed picture of laudable performance, inherent problems and hopeful prospects. There was erratic growth in National income and per capita income trends during the planning period and the market-propelled economy with a six-fold increase in per capita income in absolute terms. There were significant shifts in sectoral structure—declining share of agriculture from 56 per cent to 29 per cent and increasing share of industrial sector from 15 per cent to 29 per cent and services sector from 29 per cent to 42 per cent. The socio-economy witnessed a high rate of saving and investment and a record level of foodgrains production from 50.8 million tonnes in 1950-51 to 198 million tonnes in 1996-97 with uneven increase in the per capita availability (498 grams per day). But there was a 20-fold increase in the wholesale price index and the consumer price index. It is disheartening to note that there was a halting progress in the poverty alleviation programmes.

In August 1947, when India achieved political Independence, centralised planning was required to tackle the colonial spilled over problems of poverty, illiteracy, food deficit and industrial backwardness. Dr. M.V. Mathur (the 1967 Golden Jubilee Conference President of IEA) has proposed a non-conventional agenda to achieve more regional development and make a success of decentralised planning under Panchayati Raj. It includes the transformation of Planning Commission of Government of India into an Economic Policy Formulation Advisory Council, making Finance Commission into a Standing Commission, Coordination of the State-level Development Commissions, establishment of one more tier in decentralised planning and development at the levels of existing revenue divisions, formation of State-level Development and Finance Commissions and Development of well-coordinated linkages with educational institutions.

Primary sector and its allied activities need priority in planning and plan implementation as the agricultural sector contributes 30 per cent of GDP with 65 per cent of employment potential in India today. Apart from being an employment generator, agricultural activities should emerge as the underplanning of a welfare-oriented State under the market-friendly economy. It is imperative that more than proportionate allocation of resources should be prioritized in the Ninth Plan (1997-2002) not only in the interest of farmers but also that of the country's economy.

Dr. P.R. Brahmananda (the Diamond Jubilee Conference President) has argued in his indomitable style that the Indian planners' secondary importance to the primary sector has actually parked the country' development on the wrong side with a 'big push' towards industrialisation since the inauguration of the First Plan (1951-56). After 50 years, the resultant realities are: a widening gap in net product between agricultural and non-agricultural workers, a stagnation in the real wages of agricultural sector in the 1990s and declining farm and food growth rates despite a record level of foodgrains production in 1996-97. A new deal should depend upon agricultural fundamentalism with integrated and coordinated rural productive development programmes.

The post-Independence industrialisation is largely shaped by the predominant role of the public enterprises in many infrastructural core sectors. This is due to the weak and narrow industrial base, low levels of savings and investment and lack of infrastructure at the time of Independence. The strategy of industrialisation until 1980 broadly followed the Nehruvian model of development—a bias towards heavy-industries. Since the Sixth Plan (1980-85), the policy of liberalisation slowly has taken roots in our soil with larger participation of big industrial houses and free entry multinationals. Although there is a consensus, with the New Economic Reform measures on liberalising India's trade regime globalising its economy, serious concerns are being expressed on some of its operational aspects.

Dr. V.R. Panchamukhi (the 1994 President) has highlighted the distinct achievements of the post-Independence process of industrialisation and also its inherent weaknesses and challenges. He is emphatic that one should not lose sight of the structural factors that have been responsible for the perpetuation of the weaknesses in the industrial sector. The basic challenge before the policy-makers and the corporate sector is one of the identifying the structural factors responsible for the persistence of the weaknesses and identifying ways and means of removing them on a sector by sector basis. After 50 years the corporate sector has developed substantial strength and resilience to face the new challenges. It is necessary that the Government and the corporate sector together emerge as "India incorporated" to enable the Indian economy to fully exploit all its potential in the next fifty years. V.R. Panchamukhi also outlined a National Interest Trade Model for India. He pointed out a peculiar kind of Prisoner's Dilemma situation that is India apprehending that all other countries would "gang" upto isolate her and the other countries fearing that India would dominate them. Both of these perceptions are misconceived and are based on inadequate appreciation of the potential benefits of cooperation and also insufficient awareness of the costs of non-cooperation. India should take leadership role—not in the big brother sense, but as an effective and a benevolent patron of the region's progress taking full advantage of the economics of neighbourhood.

Infrastructural development is a conveyer-belt which facilities the speedier growth in all sectors. The country inherited a shattered railway system with overused and obsolete assets and the dislocation effect of the Partition. Today Indian Railways is the largest network in the whole world with a phenomenal increase in rolling and running stocks like routes kilometres with expanded electrified routes, steam and diesel locomotives, passenger coaches, Electrical Multiple Coaches, Wagons and high growth in freight and passenger traffic connecting Kashmir and Kanyakumari. In his thoroughgoing theoretical exercises and empirical evidence, Dr. D.M. Nanjundappa (the 1981 President) has found out that if the Indian railways adopt marginal cost pricing, they would incur a heavy deficit while average cost pricing would facilitate a marginal surplus in earnings. Against the backdrop of the huge expensive programmes and uncertain internal resource generation, it is imperative that the Indian railways finances should get restructured without any further delay to overhaul the administrative mechanism. Simultaneously, the indiscrete populist subsidies should be phased out to stabilise the financial management. If it is effected there is more scope for improvement in railways services with a lower cost.

Since 1980s the process of economic planning and its policy perspectives have hurdled over privatisation, liberalisation and globalisation strategies in India. In July 1991, the New Economic reform policy led to the adoption of the Structural Adjustment Programme with a wide-ranging package reforms in trade, industry, finance and other important sectors of the economy. Since July 1996, the 13-Political party coalition government at the Central level has adopted the Common Minimum Programme with maximum contents of reform as a framework of economic policy. At the end of six years (1991-1997), the outcome of NEP has rather been mixed. Since the introduction of economic reforms in India, the 'Course' of reforms has been subject to a series of scrutiny as well as country-wise comparative studies.

Dr. Alak Ghosh (the 1987 President) has made a comprehensive critical and comparative analysis of economic reforms in India and China with special reference to changes that have occurred in the financial sector particularly banking and insurance. China, instead of going for a 'big-bang' policy, opted for an experiment with 'gradualism' based on a selective approach. India, started with a 'big-bang' policy between July and December, 1991, but in subsequent years tilted towards 'gradualism'. China, under autocratic rule, achieved economic liberalisation without political liberalisation. India, under democratic Government scored full marks in the case of political liberalisation. But achieved only partial success in the sphere of economic liberalisation. The Indian policy-makers, during the last few years of economic reforms were forced to give a 'human face' to the reform process by substantially increasing the expenditure for the social sector to make a frontal attack on poverty and unemployment. Successes and shortfalls in banking sector will largely depend upon four basic parameters—competitive efficiency, internal strength and profitability, operational flexibility and autonomy in decision-making.

We have found that, during the reform period, the Indian banking system has achieved greater amount of competitive efficiency than the Chinese Banks. This is mainly because of intense competition between Indian banks and foreign banks for improving customer service. Further, in the case of China financial reforms, though pragmatic and impressive for a Communist country, has not followed a rigid, comprehensive blueprint. Rather, it has bee characterised by gradualism and selectivism. There are many gray areas which require immediate attention. The unfinished agenda for further financial reforms both in India and China remains highly challenging with lack of proper reforms in insurance sector.

At the 50th year of Independence, from the President of India, Prime Minister down to the presidents of Panchayats all over the country, all proclaimed that corruption is cancerous in its growth and that curatives are necessary. Corruption as an endemic evil spreading the different layers of the political system and the economy, is by means a unique Indian phenomenon. But its manifestations and ramifications—black money and black wealth accumulation, scams of all sorts and money laundering in all ways—exhibit the devalued moral values in public life. The real concern is over the distinct deterioration in the culture of governance in India to the point where developmental funding becomes almost synonymous with a gross misappropriation of public resources.

Dr. D.L. Narayana (the 1984 President) is candid, in his pathological investigation of the incidence of social and political corruption in Independent India and emphatic in his diagnostic prescriptions. Different types of corruptive practices in terms of grass eating, meat eating, institution eating, state eating and Nation eating show the percolation effect of Canker of Corruption. Corruption is most conspicuous while the percolation impact of economic growth is least visible. A National movement to combat corruptive practices should become people's agenda. It means relentless battle against power-holders, power-dealers and power-brokers in different walks of life.

We must admit the fact that the most important objectives of planning have not been achieved, the most cherished goals seem to be almost as distant today as when we set out on the road to planned development since 1951. Even the six year old (1991-97) economic reforms did not usher in a new society. Fifty years after achieving independence, poverty, illiteracy, disease and lack of minimum social services continue to affect hundreds of millions of our people.

In the next 50 years, do we need the development of few or all? Do we need an integral human development or a lop-sided development? There should be a positive people-participatory development plan well-integrated with the country's problems and potential. The ultimate goal of any type of development programme in the 21st century is to make men and women better-off in their own environment without any discrimination and deprivation. It lies in the perfection of the social order.

Vellore P. JEGADISH GANDHI

Contributors

Dr. M.V. Mathur has been Professor of Economics and Vice-Chancellor in the University of Rajasthan at Jaipur. He has served as a Member of Government of India's Third Finance Commission (1960-61), Education (Kothari) Commission (1964-66), and Fourth Central Pay Commission (1983-87). He was Chairman of Rajasthan Universities Reorganisation Committee. The President of India awarded Prof. Mathur "Padma Bhushan" for his services in the fields of Economics and Education.

Dr. P.R. Brahmananda is a leading economist of the country also internationally recognised for his contributions to welfare economics, growth, development and planning, monetary theory in the domestic and international spheres, and economics of inflation. He was the RBI Professor of Monetary Economics at the Bombay School of Economics and was also for several years its Director. He has been an editor of the "Indian Economic Journal". He is a penalist in the policy-making consultations, Government of India.

Dr. V.R. Panchamukhi is the Director, Research and Information System for the Non-Aligned and other Developing Countries (RIS), New Delhi. RIS is a forum essentially for providing analytical support to the developing countries on various international economic issues of concern to the process of their development. He was the Convenor of Steering Committee of the 8th World Economic Congress (1986), New Delhi. He is the Managing Trustee, The Indian Economic Association Trust for R & D. He is the first President of the SAARC Economic Association (SEA).

Dr. D.M. Nanjundappa is the Chairman, Indian Council of Social Science Research (ICSSR). He is the Deputy Chairman, Planning Board, Government of Karnataka. He is a member of the Disinvestment Commission, Government of India. He was Professor and Head of the Department of the Economics, Karnataka University and Vice-Chancellor of Karnataka and Bangalore Universities. He was the Secretary, Planning and Institutional Finance, Government of Karnataka and Economic Adviser to Government of Karnataka. He was the Member of Panel of Economists, Planning Commission, Government of India and Chairman, Railway Fare and Tariff Committee, Government of India.

Dr. Alak Ghosh is the President, International Institute for Development Studies. He is the Director of the Capital Market Survey Project and Member of the Expert Committee (State Finance), Planning Commission, Government of India. He was formerly Professor and Head of the Department of Economics of Calcutta University. He is the author of the popular text book 'Indian Economy: Its Nature and Problems' since 1957.

Dr. D.L. Narayana is the Emeritus Professor of Economics, Sri Venkateswara University, Triupati. He was the Chairman of the International Economic Association, 8th World Conference Organisation, New Delhi. He was the Founder of the Andhra Pradesh Economic Association. He was Chairman of the Indian Society of Labour Economics and the Editor, Indian Journal of Labour Economics. He is Trustee Member of the Indian Economic Association Trust for R & D.

CHAPTER 1

Decentralised Planning and Development—A Non-Conventional Agenda

M.V. MATHUR

On the happy occasion of celebrations of our country's 50 years of Independence, we have been provided an opportunity to reflect on our achievements and future possibilities of growth on various fronts.

It was my good fortune to have presided over the Golden Jubilee session of the Indian Economic Association in December, 1967 at Madras (now Chennai). At the time I had offered in my Presidential Address some thoughts on our framework for planning, development and union state financial relations. Happily those thoughts have not gone in vain; some of those ideas have bee put into practice. Our country's Golden Jubilee provides me a golden opportunity to put forward a further agenda-perhaps a non-conventional one-on similar issues. Our wish is that when India celebrates Platinum Jubilee of its

Independence, it can claim to have achieved more balanced regional development and make a success of decentralised planning under Panchayati Raj.

Our experience of planning and development has indicated not only the need for careful planning but also for effective administration and management. Evaluations of successive Five Year Plans have highlighted for fact that while planning had been carefully done, bottlenecks in administration at various levels could not result in implementation of desired goals. In a British text book on Elementary Economics in my intermediate classes, I had read that apart from land, labour and capital organisation and management were also important factors of production. Unfortunately, the latter two factor have not attached for attention they deserved and hence the pitfalls that we have faced in successfully carrying out of our planned programmes.

Perhaps the most important development in economic sphere in recent years has been the emergence of a liberalised economy. Obviously the role of the Planning Commission in he altered situation cannot be the same as before. However, one has not witnessed any significant changes in its methods of operations even during the post liberalised era. In a recent parliamentary debate the Prime Minister Shri I.K. Gujral has rightly stated that they do not wish to give a statutory status to the Planning Commission. While we agree with this, it is to be seen as to whether in the altered economic climate, the country's demands for development cannot be met by the full utilisation of the statutory responsibilities of a constitutional authority, viz. the Finance Commission. As originally envisaged, the Finance Commission was to provide necessary programmes, funds and mechanism for balanced regional development. It was also expected that all financial transfers from the Union to the States, 'whether revenue or capital', were to be made on the recommendations of Finance Commission. Unfortunately, the Finance Commission has not been allowed to flower in full in view of the emergence of a powerful Planning Commission. In its 'general observations', the Third Finance Commission had made certain suggestions to deal with the existence of these two bodies. One of the those suggestions later on found favour with the authorities and a member of the Planning Commission was put also as a member in successive Finance Commissions. Unfortunately, that member invariably did not remain in the Planning Commission to fully coordinate the task.

In a liberalised economy with a more federalistic polity and a multiplicity of political parties holding power in our States, it is increasingly necessary to provided an institutional set up which is more in tune with the constitutional provisions. We would, therefore, reiterate our suggestion that the Finance Commission should become a 'Standing' Commission, if not a permanent one (Details follow). Further, the existing Planning Commission should be reorganised as a similar body in the shape of an Economic Policy Advisory Council.

TRANSFORMATION OF PLANNING COMMISSION INTO AN ECONOMIC POLICY FORMULATION ADVISORY COUNCIL

In an era of liberalised economy while the need for tight control exercised by the Planning Commission diminishes, the need for well-thought out and coordinated economic policies in the spheres of industry, commerce, agriculture and foreign investment increases. The new EPAC should be under the Chairmanship of the P.M., with a full-time policy 'technocrat' as Deputy Chairman. The F.M., and not more than five experts should be its part-time Members. Ministers in-charge of Industry, Commerce, Agriculture, and Foreign Economic Affairs should be invited when their sectoral policies are under discussion.

Apart from advice regarding well-coordinated central policies, this council could also offer suggestions regarding their effective implementation at State and cutting-edge levels.

FINANCE COMMISSION

As per the spirit of the constitution it would be more desirable to provide all ascertainable flows of funds from the Centre to the States through the mechanism of the Finance Commission. For performing this task the Finance Commission has to be made a standing commission if not a permanent one. Fortunately our constitution is flexible enough to accommodate this within the existing framework of Article 280. The obligatory requirement under this Article is that the Finance Commission should be appointed by the President atleast once in 5 years. There can, therefore, be no objection if this body is brought into existence every 5 years during which period it could remain as a standing Commission and meet as often as necessary. This may of course require some changes in the composition and terms of appointment of members of the Finance Commission. Unless the work of the Commission so develops that it requires full time attention of most of the members, it would be better to have only one or two persons as full members. Others could remain as part time members and attend the meetings of the Commission as and these are convened.

For ensuring proper linkage and continuity tenure of all the members of the Finance Commission need not be co-terminus. Initially, some of the members may be appointed for a period of 2 or 3 years and the rest for a full term of 5 years. Afterwards all appointments could be for a full 5-year term. Thus, some new members will be joining the Commission every 2 or 3 years. This will provide the necessary fresh outlook from time to time while still preserving continuity in membership to a certain extent.

It should be possible for the Finance Commission to interact with political and professional technocrats for programmes of more balanced regional development. The members of State-level Development Commission should be of Special help. Discussion papers could be prepared for less developed areas or comparatively neglected sectors to bring up their development. More grants could be provided for States which for historical and other reasons had lagged behind in developing their resources. The 'advanced' States could depend on market mechanism for further enhancing their development activity.

The Finance Commission, under its Constitutional authority, could check with State authorities about utilisation of funds as agreed to earlier and also ensure that non-plan development programmes do not dry up until they reach their final goals.

PANCHAYATI RAJ INSTITUTIONS

One of the more significant achievements towards decentralised planning and development has been the recent constitutional amendment to provide for setting up of Panchayati Raj institutions in our States in the shape of village panchayats, block level samitis and District level zila parishads, and the provision of a Panchayati Raj Finance Commission to devolve funds from the States to PR institutions. Almost all the States have provided for necessary legislation to implement the provisions made for Panchayati Raj institutions in the central legislation. In several States Panchayati Raj Finance Commissions have also made their recommendations. However, in many states the necessary administrative authority for appropriate planning and development activity at the three-tier levels has yet to emerge. It is said that the members of State Legislatures, while adhering to the desire of the Centre, do not wish to lose their hold and authority in favour of the elected representatives in the three-tier Panchayati Raj. How should be resolve this dilemma? In my view, we should add another tier of decentralised planning and development at the level of existing revenue divisions (or at similar levels if the revenue divisions have formally ceased to exist). We can call this new Panchayati Raj tier, which will be below the State Assembly but above the zila parishad, by the name of Kshetriya Parishad or Regional Panchayat.

All MLA's representing this region in State Assembly should be *ex-officio* members of this Kshetriya Parishad (KP). All Chairmen of zila parishads and may be one other representative of each zila parishad in the region should be members of this body. All the Members of Parliament from the region should be permanent invitees to KP meetings so that their advice may be available for drawing up desirable development plans keeping in view past aberrations in plan implementation. The Divisional Commissioner who is very often a very senior IAS officer and who is perhaps not over-worked at present, should function as the Chief Executive Officer of this body. The members of KP should elect one of the MLAs as their Chairman unless the legislation provides for the senior most MLA to occupy this position. Hopefully, the MLAs in the State Assembly and wherever necessary the MP's in the Parliament will carefully watch the interest of development of this region and try to avoid all the bottlenecks in implementation. They should be able to provide better informed guidance to Zila Parishads and act as their spokesmen in the Assembly and with the State Government. The Kshetriya Parishad will be a useful Coordinating agency and a significant brain-storming forum. Except for a limited number of inter-Zila Parishad development programmes, the rest of the programmes will be carried out under the auspices of the Zila Parishads.

A very important corollary for effective implementation of Panchayati Raj plans will be to decentralise State level administrative and allied services.

The members of the State services should be recruited by the State Public Service Commission on a competitive basis and, on the basis of their-preference and performance, allotted to one of the regions of the State so that by and large major part of their career is spent in the region, part from some postings at the State Headquarters (this should be somewhat on the pattern of recruitment of members of IAS who are centrally recruited and then assigned to States). The regional authorities should have major control over the functioning of the services in their respective areas. Thus, it should be possible for the Panchayati Raj institutions to have the much needed coordination between elected representatives in the existing 3-tiers and the elected representatives in the State Assembly and the Central Parliament together with appropriate control over senior civil service to ensure Proper implementation of development programmes. Appropriate authority and control over subordinate services and staff should be formally devolved at the other tiers of Panchayat Raj.

STATE LEVEL DEVELOPMENT AND FINANCE COMMISSION

At present some States have provided for State level Planning Commissions or Planning Boards and some others have Planning Advisory Bodies. State like Kerala, Tamil Nadu and West Bengal have provided for a full time Deputy Chairman or Vice-Chairman and some full time members of these Commissions, the Chief Minister of the State being invariably the Chairman of these bodies. We would like to suggest that all States should provide for a State level Development and Finance Commission with several full time members assigned with responsibilities for key sectors of development in the State. This body should be responsible for developmental planning, non-plan development activity and flow of funds from the State level to the various tiers of Panchayati Raj institutions. If necessary, to implement statutory provisions of Panchayati Raj legislation, some members of the Commission could be constituted as Panchayati Raj Finance Commission when the occasion arises. This combination of triple functions is necessary to avoid the existing purely accounting distinction between 'plan' and 'non-plan' developmental activities and their much needed coordination between the State level and the various tiers of Panchayati Raj institutions. This will also provide professional coordination between the Central and State authorities and continuing overseeing of development activities not only for a plan period of five years but as long as proper carrying out of even 'non-plan' development demands.

The members of DFCs will be in a much better position to put forward their claims, well-supported by technical papers, before the Finance Commission. As Finance Commission will be available all along, it should be possible to plug holes in effective implementation as soon as these are discovered.

State DFCs should also ensure that appropriate machinery for planning and implementation is in place in the Z.P., P.S., and Panchayats.

LINKAGES WITH EDUCATIONAL INSTITUTIONS

We suggest that for improved planning and development, Universities, Professional and 'General' Colleges, Polytechnics, and senior secondary institutions should be optimally linked with various tiers of Panchayatiraj bodies, specially for purposes of basic surveys, orientation and training of PR staff and NGO personnel, and evaluation of plan-programmes. In many cases the teaching staff of these institutions happen to be the best available 'brain-power' under one institutional roof in the area of PR tier concerned but we have not fully utilised and moulded this human resource. They can help in natural and human resource surveys in villages and townships, putting forward candidate' programmes of development in selected sectors, and writing out 'development' manuals at micro levels. They could also perform a useful role in carrying out 'evaluations' of completed or ongoing programmes at village and Samiti levels. In the process these College teachers will enrich their own knowledge and become more 'relevant and proficient teachers'.

CONCLUSION

We have offered a some-what non-traditional agenda, within the framework of existing Constitution, to devolve more authority, responsibility and opportunity for innovative thinking for decentralised development to succeed. It is our belief that when action is taken nearer the people the possibility of dealing more effectively with problems of poverty, illiteracy and disease increases. Action on the lines proposed in this short article can be one of the best 'gifts' in the Celebration of fifty years of India's Independence.

CHAPTER

2

Primary Sector: Performance, Problems and Perspectives

P.R. BRAHMANANDA

Agriculture is important in a number of respects in a developing economy such as India with large population size and high population growth rate. Agriculture is the primary source directly and indirectly, of food, which is necessary for the subsistence of the population. Since the economy is subject to droughts and famines, there must be enough food stocks to enable subsistence in lean periods.

Human beings as labour require more than subsistence to work efficiently. Hence, the requirement of output/supply of food articles must be more than what is required for bare subsistence. So also, more stocks are necessary to provide for contingencies. Agriculture is the primary source of raw materials and process products which form an important part, directly or indirectly, of non-food wage-goods such as cloth, milk, meat, vegetable oils, sugar and so on. Agriculture is the primary source of feed for livestock and dairy, animals. It is also, directly and indirectly, a primary source of exports. Agriculture is equally important a source of livelihood for the larger portion of the population and the labour force. Those who are not employed in factories and services in urban areas have to depend upon agriculture for their occupations, main or subsidiary. It is the reserve of the vast million of the disguised unemployed. In the years prior to the first World War, land revenue, constituting about 2 per cent of NDP, was the leading source of tax revenues.

There is a school of thought, which flourished in France in the 17th and 18th centuries, known as Agricultural Fundamentalism, which considered agriculture as the basic—or the most basic-economic activity. It is in agriculture and related activities that the output is also the primary input for the above activities. In the case of the other sectors, the exchange of products has to occur with agriculture and related activities, on which they are dependent. Agriculture was deemed productive, whereas other activities—including manfuacturing—and services (including Government services)—were deemed sterile. This was because the latter could not supply inputs to agriculture. If farmers did not demand non-agricultural products and Government services, these would not come into existence at all.

Ricardo, the great founder of classical economic theory, enlarged the concept of fundamentalism to encompass the category of wage-goods. Wage-goods are those consumption goods which are purchased/consumed by labour to enable the subsistence work. The wage-goods are included in the conventional real wage. Later, Karl Marx included activities in other sectors supplying direct and indirect inputs to wage-goods, also as fundamental or basic.

The concept of integrated wage-goods formalises the above approach. Here, no activity can be performed without labour, directly or indirectly. Hence, wage-goods and inputs for the same are all basic. Luxury goods, machinery and so on, intended for expansion for its own sake, are not basic. Only that portion of fixed capitals which enters as inputs in wage-goods in basic. Not all heavy industries are, therefore, basic. This distinction is very important in determining the pattern of investment in a developing economy.

Agriculture and related activities are included in the integrated wage-goods because they are the source of wage-goods directly or indirectly. The integrated wage-goods concept encompasses both agriculture and components of manufacturing and essential services. It excludes heavy industries intended for the self-same expansion and luxury goods. The latter, again, are deemed so because of conventions and as they would not be entering the wage-goods basket given the real wage.

Neo-classical economics treats all consumption goods as basic, so all commodities which are used in the production of consumption goods in the present/future do not become basic in neo-classical theory. Capital, itself, is so defined as implying the capacity to produce consumption goods in future.

In the early stages of development and in a poor economy with a large population, the entire labour force does not get employment at a reasonably full real wage and for the whole of the year. Thus there is no triple-full employment in a country such as India. Triple-full employment is conditional upon the pre-existence of capacity to supply that quantity of wage-goods as would be required for such employment. It is because of the huge gap in such capacity that we cannot transform the Indian economy to a state of zero absolute poverty and triple-full employment. It is because of our inadequate production capacity in agriculture and related activities that such transformation has not been possible.

In post-Independence India, our planners, though paying lip service to agriculture; actually treated agriculture as peripheral. Even ministers at State and Centre—not excluding Prime Ministers and Chief Ministers—hardly realised the close link between full employment, poverty eradication and agricultural growth.

Let me repeat that in both the classical and the Marxian models, as also the integrated wage-goods model, agriculture becomes a most important basic activity. This is so till the stage when all potential units of labour are able to get employment at minimal wage-goods and for the whole of the year. The gap in respect of capacity to produce sufficient integrated wage-goods is the primary reason for poverty and unemployment. It should follow, therefore, that for quite some years to come, agricultural fundamentalism—or, rather, wage-good fundmentalism—has an important theoretical and practical significance in our economy with large poverty and large unemployment.

Unfortunately, in India, the thinking of the establishment has been to imitate western models of development in which the indutrialisation process got dominant attention. Jawaharlal Nehru was influenced largely by the Soviet model of industrialisation, with emphasis on heavy industries. In the famous Feldman model, which lay at the back of the Stalinist economic model, the output of wage-good and of agricultural commodities was kept constant and all savings, even in a gross sense, were ploughed back for heavy industry development.

This pattern emphasised the network of activities consisting of machine-building, heavy transport, mining and related infrastructure such as electricity. The forward expansion of production of final consumer goods, which would have consisted mostly of agricultural commodities, was not the goal of planning. At the same time, following the thesis of Probrianzski, industrial goods were to be sold to agriculturists at high prices, thus turning the terms of trade against them.

Mahalanobis produced a model similar to that of Feldman. This appealed to Nehru and the strategy of development visualised in the Second Plan was forced on the economy. Even the Leftist economists treated Marx in a naive manner. They interpreted the Stalinist model as tantamount to Marxist theory in practice. We added two other components: Deficit financing and an over-valued exchange-rate. Agricultural development and infrastructure for the same got naturally neglected. The massive PL 480 food inflow also made us neglect the need for domestic agricultural growth. The two drought years of 1965 and 1966 made us partly recover our lost sights.

The Green Revolution came along with the devaluation of the rupee and the establishment of the Agricultural Prices Commission. The devaluation made food imports excessively prohibitive and the development strategy had to be changed. It was at this time that we suddenly became aware of the huge measure of poverty of our people who had barely enough access to food to meet even marginal requirements of subsistence. It was shown that poverty eradication had to place cardinal emphasis on food and agricultural production. The heavy industries strategy could not have led to increased supplies of food and agricultural commodities.

By the mid-1960s, we had exhausted the scope for bringing new area under cultivation. Further development required massive investments in irrigation, heavy consumption of fertilisers and adoption of high yielding seeds. The growth of agricultural production from 1967-68 was largely obtained through sustained rising trend in yields. The three inputs—water, fertilisers and high equality seeds—have helped avoid famines, without resort to food imports. Between 1949-50 and 1995-96, the growth rate of food production was about 2.5 per cent per annum, the growth rate of area, a half per cent per annum, and the growth rate of yields, 2 per cent per annum. Since no more growth of area is possible in the future, we have to depend primarily upon sustaining a high trend in yields. The growth rate of non-food grains production over the last 46 years was about 2.9 per cent per annum. The growth rate of area here has been 1.3 per cent per annum and the growth rate of yields slightly more than 1 per cent per annum. The growth rate of agricultural production in the post-Independence period has been about 2.6 per cent annum, whereas the growth in area has been 0.7 per cent per annum and that in yield 1.9 per cent. It may be noted that the growth in yields has been lower than that in population. This is no in regard to both food and non-food commodities. In the post-Green Revolution period, yield growth has our saviour. Can this be maintained? And if so, for how long?

GROWING NET-PRODUCT GAP

One of the important results of a strong and optimal

priorities-oriented development process is that, from Census to Census, the proportion of workforce to total work-force dependent upon agriculture and allied activities should go on declining and the disparities between the per-worker product in agriculture and allied activities and in the rest of the economy, as reflected in national accounts, should become narrower. According to the classical pattern of development agriculture and allied activities should get dominant priority in the pattern of investment and other efforts in the early stage of development. Thereafter, at the second stage, the sector of manufacturing and related activities should get preferential allocations. In the third stage, the tertiary sector—consisting of transport, communications, trade, professional and other services, real estates and government activities-should get priority attention. Thus, the relative accent of emphasis on the three groups of activities would keep shifting through time. If one assumes that with Independence the real development process began in right earnest, it seems that priority attention was placed on manufacturing before the agriculture stage was crossed. Further, before the manufacturing stage was completed, the switch over to the tertiary, or the services stage was made. Consequently, there have been severe distortions in the growth of the per capita net product in the three groups.

After Independence, around 1951, 72 per cent of the workforce was dependent on agriculture and related activities, the latter consisting of livestock, forestry, fishing, hunting, plantations and horticulture, among others. In 1961 and 1971, the proportion remained more or less the same. In 1981 the production slightly declined to 69 per cent. In 1991 the proportion was about 67 per cent. The proportion of cultivators, which was 50 per cent in 1951, went up to 53 per cent in 1961. And from 1971 onwards, it has been declining (in 1971, 43 per cent; in 1981, 42 per cent and in 1991, 38 per cent). But the proportion of agricultural labour, 20 per cent and 17 per cent in 1951 and 1961, rose sharply in 1961. In 1971 it was 26 per cent, in 1981, 25 per cent and in 1991, it was again 26 per cent. There may be partly statistical reasons for the sharp rise in 1961. But while the proportion of cultivators has been falling, the proportion of agricultural labour has moved up. Even regarding the later, the proportion of casual labour has moved up in relation to regular, contractual labour. It is interesting that the land reforms, ostensibly aimed at improving the lot of labour in agriculture, have tended to actually worsen their lot.

The objectives of passionate ideology can be defeated if they are not imbibed with practical economics. If at all one group has consistently suffered the worst in our development process, it is the class of agricultural labourers, which in 1991 amounted to 74 millions—about 4 times the number of organised, unbanised labour, so assiduously cultivated by trade unions an the Left parties. Small and marginal farmers, who have also been affected by the development process, have been excluded. Their numbers also constitute millions.

In 1950-51, the relative share of agricultural and allied activities in net national production in 1980-81 prices was 49 per cent. In 1960-61 it came down to 46 per cent; in 1970-71 it slid further to 40 per cent; and in 1980-81 it had fallen to 35 per cent. In 1990-91 this figure further declined to 29 per cent, and in 1996-97 it was about 28 per cent. Over nearly 50 years, the relative share of agriculture and allied activities dropped by 44 per cent, whereas the relative share of the workforce in them has declined only by less than 6 per cent. Further, the relative share of agriculture and related activities in net product has been declining more or less continuously, whereas the modest decline in the relative share in workforce is only in the recent periods. Consequently, the ratio of per worker net product in agriculture to that in the rest of the economy has been falling. In 1950-51, it was 68 per cent in 1960-61, 64 per cent; in 1970-71, 56 per cent; in 1980-81, 51 per cent; and in 1990-91, 43 per cent. Probably in 1996-97 it would have been about 40 per cent. The ratio thus fell by about 42 per cent in the post-Independence period. The rate of growth of per worker product in agriculture has been going up at a lower rate in non-agriculture over the post-Independence and post-Plan era. The real wages in agriculture have been going up at the lower ate than in non-agriculture. In fact, there has been stagnation thus far in the 1990s in the real wage. The minimum wages in rural areas have been only on paper.

The real wage in agriculture has probably been going up at a lower rate than the growth rate of yields, at least in recent years. Probably the income distribution pattern in agriculture has been getting skewed, particularly in prosperous areas. This does not mean that the Green Revolution has not benefited agricultural labour and small and marginal farmers. Their conditions would have been more severely and adversely affected had the Green Revolution not taken place. In fact, in areas where the Green Revolution's effects have been sparse, the conditions of the above categories of workers have improved relatively little compared to the conditions of the above categories of workers in the Green Revolution—benefited areas. The bulk of India's poor are in the above two categories of workers. If we add workers in the handloom textile sector to the above category, we would probably find most of the poor and most of the illiterate among them and their families. The condition of women in these categories is worse than that of the men.

What are the reasons for the widening gap in net product for worker between agriculture and non-agriculture? This issue has not been discussed adequately in literature. Dr. V.K.R.V. Rao, in his address to the World Economic Congress in 1986, touched on the above theme but did not elucidate the reasons for the growing gap. The late Prof. Dandekar also used to harp on the above theme, but he too did not go into the causes thereof. Dr. Thamarajakshi, in her book *Intersectoral Relationship in a Developing Economy—The Indian Experience* (New Delhi 1994) has drawn attention to the relation between the declining net barter terms of trade between the prices of agricultural commodities and the prices of inputs for agricultural production. In his comprehensive presidential address in 1996 to the conference of the Indian Society of Agricultural Economics, Dr. S.S. Acharya has given a wide range of data regarding prices, costs and incomes to throw light on the lower rate of relative improvement of people dependent on agriculture, *vis-a-vis* the workers dependent on other activities.

It may be worthwhile outlining the probable causes for the growing gap eluded earlier.

- The growth rate agricultural production in the post-Independence period has been lower than that in non-agriculture.
- Whereas physical and human capital are important sources for value-added in industry and allied services, land is the important sources of value-added in agriculture. Land area has not been increasing whereas capital stock has been increasing.
- Capital and infrastructure for agriculture have grown at a lower rate than those required for industry, etc. The human capital application in agriculture has been limited. Even primary education is not universal in rural areas.
- The burden of disguised unemployment has been borne mostly by agriculture. There has been some migration from rural to urban areas but the barriers to movement of surplus labour in agriculture to activities outside agriculture and across regions are quite strong. These barriers have been growing more and more unpiercable.
- Production systems in agriculture continue to be characterised by small and marginal farms in most of India. Instead of planning for the removal of surplus labour through planned capital formation programmes, India pursued the policy of encouraging smaller and smaller sized farms, thus discouraging labour mobility. The employment guarantee scheme and similar schemes also made labour immobile.
- The growth of crop productivity has occurred in a few portions of India. A small portion of farms produce the bulk of the marketable surplus.
- Crop productivity in dry areas has been heavily neglected.
- The terms of trade have not been in favour of agriculture. Not all crops get the full benefit of public purchase at convenient prices. Farms are still exposed to the incidence of fluctuations in prices due to vagaries in production.
- The sources of non-farm employment in rural areas

have also not expanded in a big way. The pressure on agriculture continues.

- There is a significant growth of casual employment in agriculture. This is due to mechanisation, hidden evasions of ceilings, substitution of family labour with outside labour, the unreality of minimum wages, etc.
- Inflation has relative adversely affected workers in agriculture more than workers in other sectors. Agricultural prices in recent years have risen at a lower rate than general prices.

DECLINING FARM AND FOOD GROWTH RATES

Between 1950-51 and 1996-97, the growth rate of agricultural production—at 2.8 per cent— was above the population growth rate of 2.1 per cent. But between 1990-91 and 1996-97, at 2.4 per cent, it was only slightly above population growth rate of 1.9 per cent. While the growth rate of food production, at 2.9 per cent, was slightly above the population growth rate, between 1990-91 and 1996-97 it fell to 1.3 per cent—substantially less than the population growth rate. In most crops, there has been declaration in the growth rates 1990-91 onwards. The position regarding cereals (rice and coarse) and pulses is truly alarming, as also that of total foodgrains. Pulses are the primary source of proteins for the majority of the population. There are widespread reports that the soil fertility for sugarcane is declining. While jute is almost dying, tobacco is stationary. Improvements are noticed in oilseeds, potato, cotton and coconut. Non—foodgrains, as a whole, are growing at a higher ratethan the population. Taking all crops, the growth rate of 2 per cent in the most recent period is a sure sign of the declining growth rate in agriculture. Particularly so, because of the excellent monsoons in this period.

One explanation is provided in the declining growth rate of fertiliser consumption. The growth rate of irrigated area is also falling. That the overall crop production growth rate is declining at a higher rate than the above in the most recent period should be s serious cause for concern to those who care about the future of Indian agriculture. The successive Five-Year Plans, barring the Fifth, revealed a wide gap between the actual and target growth of foodgrains and most other crops. During the Sixth Plan, as against the goal of 154 million tonnes, the terminal production was 146 million tonnes. In the Seventh Plan, against a target of 183 million tonnes, the achievement was 171 million tonnes. In the Eighth Plan, while the goal was 210 million tonnes, just 191 million tonnes was reached. There are similar shortfalls in cotton, jute and oilseeds. The planners, God bless them, are targeting for the Ninth Plan a growth rate of agricultural crops of above 4 per cent and of food crops of above 3 per cent; and this given the achievement of less than half the above rate during the Eighth Plan. None of the Chief Ministers, let alone the then Prime Minister, seem to have been concerned about the nitty gritty of the targeted growth rates in the face of such poor achievement. Whether the rulers are concerned or not, the future of Indian agriculture is grim. On the one hand, the burden of government responsibility for supplying rations is increasing. The goal of eradicating poverty through the revamped PDS necessitates higher foodgrains production. On the other hand, the actual performance and the prospects are well below the norms desired by the authorities.

At the same time, the proportion of agricultural exports to agricultural output has risen, and gains, especially rice, are being merrily exported. Import of wheat in large quantities has begun. Target fixation planning has been abolished. Have we realised the cumulate consequences of all these contradictions in the context of a probable decline in the agricultural growth rate? There is a school of thought which believes that he calorie-based poverty line approach should be abandoned. This school believes that the poor are already so much better of that they have shifted to non-food expenditure. The income elasticity of demand, for foodgrains seems to be falling and, hence, this school argues that the target growth rate of foodgrains production should be lowered. There has been something seriously wrong in the way the growth of commodities has been planned.

There are two ways of determining the projected demand for foodgrains and other consumption necessities or essential wage-goods. The first approach is to postulate different values of the growth rates of real national income and then work out the growth rate of demand for essential wage-goods on the basis of estimates of income elasticities of demand for the latter. The second approach is to project alternative values of the growth rate of employment and then derive the growth rates of wage-goods on the basis of employment elasticity of demand for wage-goods. The second approach can be modified by bringing in a concept of desired real wage rates for workers. In the first approach, the growth rates of demand for foodgrains would be lower than in the second. A third approach, which is a variant of the second, would be to postulate different values of growth rates of wage-goods and work out projected growth rates of employment under alternative values of the real wage rate. In both the second and third approaches, the growth rate of income will be secondarily derived.

Some broad generalisations can be made: The higher the growth rates of employment targeted and the higher the levels of conventional real wages desired, the higher will be the growth rates of demand for wage-goods. Consequently, the derived demands for different types and lines of investments will be determined, as also the different quantities of various inputs required. Since agricultural commodities are essential components of wage-goods, the growth rate of agricultural output will also tend to be higher in the second and the third approaches.

In the first approach, by proceeding on the basis of historical employment elasticities of income, a lower growth rate of demand for wage-goods and of agricultural commodities such as foodgrains and other food articles will be obtained. It is necessary to abandon the first approach and move to the second and third approaches. Only then can the shortages of capacities in fertilizers, irrigation, and so on be accounted for. A fundamental change will have to emerge in the planning pattern, with a bold shift towards employment orientation. It this approach, the growth rate of income will also tend to be substantially higher.

It is necessary to note the that the supplies of wage-goods

and agricultural commodities have to be projected and planned for from outside the constrains of the income elasticity approach. The employment growth rate will have to be autonomously inducted into future planning goals. In the past, target for growth rates of heavy industry products were autonomously provided. Later, the income elasticity approach was brought in. Both these types of models underplayed the required growth rates of agricultural commodities and wage-goods. Consequently, the commodity implications of agricultural and employment growth were played down. Rural development schemes are primarily cash and income transfer schemes without the component of expansions in production and capital formation. Even then, there has not been any worthwhile rural development.

A NEW DEAL: AGRICULTURAL FUNDAMENTALISM

Indian thinking on agricultural development in the post-Independent era has evolved in a rather confused manner along several related, but often contradictory, strands. Adhocism has been the hallmark of thinking in this respect. In the early 1950s, attention was mostly on short-period, grow more food, schemes. In the First Plan, the focus was on methods for maximum procurement, land reforms and land re-organisation measures to achieve the goals of optimum-sized farms through re-distribution of holdings, land reclamation and spread of area under cultivation. Proposals for collective and co-operative farming were mooted. But the lobby for small peasants was quite strong, thanks to agricultural economists such as Prof. M.L. Dantwala.

In the Second Plan, because of the massive PL 480 food assistance from the US, the growth of food and agricultural output and investment allocations for the same got a short shift, with all attention on integrated heavy industry development. In the wake of severe droughts in 1965 and 1966 and the huge imports that had to be arranged, and with America's reluctance to bail out India from a sort of a triage prospect, Indian authorities started paying attention to rapid growth in food and agricultural production through the induction of the joint triple inputs (water, fertilisers and hybrid seeds) to land. Thus, the Green Revolution made its entry into India, because of the initiative, though against considerable unpopularity, taken by Mr. C. Subramaniam, strongly supported by T.A. Pai. We were late by 8-10 years. However, thereafter, rapid progress was made. The early 1970s to the mid-1980s saw a remarkable expansion in irrigation, fertiliser consumption and popularisation of hybrid seeds. It was in the mid-1970s that the concept of rural development was brought in, primarily by Gandhians such as Morarji Desai, Raj Krishna, Dr. Lakdawala and Dr. J.D. Sethi. Charan Singh, probably the only agricultural fundamentalist in the Indian political scene, brought in subsidies for fertilisers as an incentive for larger food production. At the same time, because of the initiative of Indira Gandhi, a number of partly anti-poverty schemes such as IRDP were introduced.

A major initiative in rural development was taken by Mr. Ramakrishna Hegde who introduced the panchayat scheme as a component of decentralised economic administration and planning. In the last year, under Mr. Deve Gowda's initiative, a minimum basic needs programme was launched. Reference should also be made to the innovation of the employment guarantee scheme such as the Lead Bank and Regional Rural Banks with credit prioritisation for agriculture. Thus, India has the experience of a wide variety of programmes and schemes, all aimed at agricultural and rural development.

But the pity is that the share of agriculture continues to decline in national and per capita product. The proportion of people below the poverty line continues to be above 40 per cent in the rural areas. Wide differentials exist between rural and urban areas, especially among women, in respect of food consumption, education, schooling facilities, access to drinking water, sanitation, roads, and health care facilities, fair price shops, and so on. Further, there has been no co-ordination in the above schemes.

What are the reasons? The different schemes have no co-ordination or integration and no overall conception. Also, there are several implementation authorities, with hardly any overall monitoring. First, the commodity aspects of agricultural development have not been incorporated in the planning models and efforts. Most agricultural economists have not pursued agricultural economics as a basic study for development and strongly feel industrialisation is the only way out. They have looked at terms of trade as a primary instruments for augmenting incomes of surplus producers. Their attitudes have to change if the economy is to emerge as a strong economic community. There have been different interpretations for the neglect of agriculture in India. One school has attribute this to the emergence of differentials in the access to certain categories of services in the rural areas. These services have been specified as: (i) absence of supply of public safe drinking water facilities; (ii) absence of minimal schooling facilities at the elementary level; (iii) absence of approach roads to villages; (iv) deficiency of minimal medical and health care services; (v) absence of public power supply for rural homes in all villages; and (vi) absence of public support for rural hosing for all sections of people in villages.

There is no reference to provision of full employment in the rural areas. It has been pointed out that the concept of rural development should emphasis public provision of the above needs, termed as basic. At the operational level, this boils down to expenditure provisions in the budgets of Central and State Government for the above purposes.

Another school lays emphasis on several types of anti-poverty programmes, some of which include expansion of employment facilities. These schemes now encompass the revamped Public Distribution System (PDS), in which all those below the poverty line are expected to get certain quantities of ration at substantially lower prices than the usual issue prices and, of course, their market prices. It is believed that the real poor can be identified in the revamped system. What is not realised is that the supplies need no necessarily lead to larger consumption by the real poor, for there is always scope for re-sale by the purchasers to those above the poverty line. Second, given the lower purchasing power with the real poor, there is always the possibility that they may not be able to purchase the provisions even if they are heavily subsidised. There is a marginal relation between the supplies through the PDS and reduction in poverty. The ultimate beneficiaries generally do not turn out to be the real poor. This is apart from the rather inadequate coverage of the PDS itself, especially in respect of States with a high proportion of people below the poverty line. The fact is the neither the minimum needs programme nor the revamped PDS, aimed at removing poverty and augmenting employment on the sustained basis, has any direct impact on employment or poverty eradication. The traditional anti-poverty schemes belong to the category of safety net programmes, which, anyway, do not form part of the mainstream of development policies and programmes. Obviously, the chief constraint on the scale of the above programmes will be the supplies of wage-goods and at low cost. This is where agricultural commodity growth becomes a primary goal. Such growth will have to processed at a rate higher than the conventional 2.5-3 per cent. The food growth rate will have to be lifted up from the current 2 per cent or less to 4 per cent per annum. The agricultural growth rate will have to be increased from 3 per cent to 5 per cent. The required infrastructure should be worked out with the above rates in mind.

Actually, if the above plans are implemented, the overall growth rates can move to 9-10 per cent, on an annual basis, for several years ahead. At the same time, as the awareness about family planning expands with education, birth rates can be brought down sooner than in the current policies. Consequently, the per capita income will rise year by year, close to 8-9 per cent per annum. A mistake in our economic policy has been to treat anti-poverty schemes as an end in themselves. The best anti-poverty scheme is that of employment expansion geared to expansion in capital formation, year by year. The removal of surplus labour from agriculture and related occupations has to be linked to capital formation programmes. The concept of capital can be expanded to include specific expenditures on training and employment in expansions of elementary education, rural public works, expansion of health, medical care and family planning services, social forestry, rural transport, tank renovations, irrigation canals, command area development, infrastructures for drinking water supply, rural libraries, rural sanitation facilities and low-cost housing. Such schemes of capital formation can be come a continuous process, and the labour transferred from agriculture can be easily absorbed by them. Along with the above schemes, there will be a need for expanding trading activities, including construction of stores and delivery depots. The scheme of panchayat raj provides scope for planning the above capital formation schemes on an integrated basis. For most of rural India, thee is vast scope for the above sort of investments. The above schemes can be substituted against the PDS wherever the beneficiaries overlap.

The so-called basic needs in planning have been delinked from capital formation and related productive expansion schemes. Even the employment guarantee scheme treats employment without linking the latter with programmes of capital formation and of income generation. Our approach has been primarily *adhoc*. The entire gamut of basic needs must be integrated with the goal of expansion in productive employment and capital formation with related recurring income-generation schemes. Agricultural fundamentalism must be integrated and coordinated with rural productive development. This approach seeks to simultaneously augment productive capital stock, employment, income, along with services of education, health and family planning.

CHAPTER 3

Trends in Industry and Trade: An Overview

V.R. PANCHAMUKHI

PROCESS OF INDUSTRIALISATION

Completion of 50 years of Independence is indeed a great milestone in the economic history of the Indian Industry. It is also an occasion for reflection on the successes and the failures as on the emerging challenges for the next 50 years.

The achievements of the process of indsustrialisation in the Indian economy has three distinct dimensions: Creation of a very wide and comprehensive industrial base; emergence of a strong and larger entrepreneurial class; and significant expansion of professionally qualified and skilled manpower. These achievements have been possible thanks to the adoption of the approach of planning for industrial transformation in the framework of import-substitution.

On the side of the negative elements of the process of

industrialisation, one may single out the following three dimension: Persistence of low levels of productivity and low scales of production compared to the other countries even in the developing world growing mis-match between the growth profiles of the different sectors, in particular between the infrastructural and the other segments; persistence of technological obsolescence and inability of the corporate sector to reach the new technological horizons.

It has now become customary to criticise the Nehruvian model of developing which emphasised the strategy of industrialisation for creating many inefficiencies. This critique of the strategy of industrialisation adopted in India since the 1950s is based on an inadequate appreciation of positive effects that have been realised over the past 50 years.

Often it is argued that the aforesaid weaknesses of the Indian industrial sector are largely because the industry has been over-protected and that too for long. It is, therefore, advocated that the induction of a competitive environment, both at the national and the international levels would shake up industry to improve its efficiency. Thus, the recent package of economic reforms includes the strategies of globalisation, liberalisation and privatisation—GLIP strategy, to put it in a nutshell.

While there is considerable truth in this argument, one should not lose sight of the real structural factors that have been responsible for the perpetuation of the weaknesses in the industrial sector. The basic challenge before the policy-makers and the corporate sector is one of identifying the structural factors responsible for the persistence of the weaknesses and identifying ways and means of removing them on a sector by sector basis.

In this context, the adoption of an unqualified strategy of globalisation, liberalization and privatisation for all the sectors as also for all sections of society in the different stages of development and for all the regions may not be the right solution. The GLIP strategy should be applied strategically and selectively.

Despite the emergence of a strong and multifaced corporate sector after 50 years of development, there is now a hue and cry to condemn the industry, the corporate sector and even the process of industrialisation itself as something totally inferior to whatever is available from the multinationals. This obsession with eulogising anything foreign is creating a crisis of confidence in the Indian corporate sector which may have far-reaching adverse implication for the future growth of the indigenous industries.

Condemning everything Indian and eulogising everything foreign is reminiscent of the attitudes during the colonial era or during the period immediately after Independence. This attitude needs to change, quickly. It is, in fact, necessary to generate an environment in which the corporate sector would be enthused to become multinationals and raise the scale of operation to be able to compete not only at home but also at the global level. The new slogan for the next decades should be "Create Indian multinationals and catch-up with the global multinationals".

The new industrial and trade environment is the global economy is characterised by four types of revolutions: Market or systemic revolution, technological, information and organisational. These revolutions themselves imply the various challenges the Indian industry would face in the next few decades.

The market or systemic revolution implies that the role of the market forces, both at the national and the international levels, has been increasing by leaps and bounds. That the market characteristics in the different market segments differ widely, leaves no hope that the unleashing of the market forces would generate a free and fair competitive environment the world-over.

Further, given the wide differences in the level of economic power of the different agents in the market and given the inadequacies of the regulatory and monetary mechanisms, the relatively more powerful agents would sway the market in their favour against the weaker ones. It is in this background that one should note that the "aggressive unilateralism" of the US has been increasing in the recent years. Further, in order to influence the nature of the effective market access opportunities, there is a growing demand for harmonisation of the economic systems in different parts of the world.

Again, the economically more powerful ones would like to impose their standards, institutions, laws, and distribution system on all others. The challenge before the policy-makers and the industry is one of preparing for these new pressure of harmonisation in standards and practices.

Information revolution would leave many economic agents of the economy marginalised unless the infrastructure for information flows, dissemination and adaption is strengthened and the facilities for training and economic agents for the new environment are made widespread. The corporate sector or, for that matter, the decision-making entities in the economy are at least more than a decade behind schedule in their preparedness to take advantage of the new opportunities provided by informatics. It is a pity that despite the acknowledgment of the superior Indian talent in the software sector, the country is still way behind.

The global technological revolution provides many suggestions for a radical shift in the corporate strategy. There should be increasing importance to R&D activity in all sectors, so that the preparedness to adapt the technologies developed elsewhere and also to innovate is strengthened. Government policies and corporate strategies should give priority to R&D activities. It may be useful to be selective in this regard so that the limited resources are put to effective use. Biotechnology, micro-electronics, software development, and solar energy could be some select areas where the indigenous R&D activity is launched on a massive scale so that India can in, say, a decade from now occupy a place of prominence in the world of technology.

There is subtle challenge which is often not recognised by the corporate sector. This is in the rapid changes taking place in industrial organisation. There is now a growing debate over a shift from the traditional Taylorist form of industrial organisation towards the new flexible forms.

In the latter, the "one-man, one-job" principle is more strident than in the former. It is also argued that the emergence of industrial clusters, wherein competition and cooperation co-exist, would provide a new framework for efficient industrial growth. The corporate sector would have to rise to these new challenging opportunities of industrial organisation to foster its competitive position on the world industrial map.

I have tried to give in a conceptual frame the specific new challenges the Indian industry would fare in the coming decades. These challenges will manifest themselves in the various forms. For instance, the new multilateral rules for trade, investment, technology transfer and services in the GATT/WTO framework and the continued negotiations that are envisaged in the WTO fora would be the venue for extensive debates on these challenges.

The country's preparedness for negotiations in the WTO and other forms needs to be strengthened jointly by the Government and the corporate sector. The pressure for phasing out the quantitative restrictions, the demand for opening-up of the service sectors and the obligation for the adoption of new rules for technology transfer indicate that industry will be facing many unexpected challenges.

The corporate sector has developed substantial strength and resilience to face the new challenges. However, there is no room of complacency in a world characterised by uncertainties and power games. It is necessary that the Government and the corporate sector together emerge as "India incorporated" to enable the Indian economy fully exploit all its potential.

A NATIONAL INTEREST MODEL FOR INDIA*

How shuld India respond to the changing world economic

* Excerpts from the presidential Address to the 76th Annual Conference of the IEA, Bombay, (1994).

situation? What would be the nature and the scope of policy interventions, while the system is being transformed to a market economy paradigm? What are the national interests which need to be protected and promoted at any cost? What are the issues related to the problem of "Level Playing Field"? These are the specific questions that haunt the economists and the policy markets. At the outset we should make a distinction between policy instruments and policy objectives. Globalisation, Marketisation and Privatisation—the three main pillars of the reforms process,—should be recognised as the instruments to achieve national interest and not as goals in themselves. I do now want to suggest that national interests are marginalised as of today. But we should recognise that the excessive fervour for policy instruments rather than for policy goals could force us to miss the woods for the trees. The current debate in the Indian Policy system has been over-obsessed by the instruments of policy, while the objectives of economic transformation are marginalised. I would illustrate this point with the example of privatisation. It is obvious that privatisation could be one of the instruments and not a goal in itself. The cherished goals is one of improving efficiency in production and marketing. In order to ensure that privatisation would bring about the cherished results of improvement in efficiency, we have to prepare a package of policies, which would facilitate the achievements of efficiency through the route of privatisation. Using this logic fully, one could proclaim that public sector can also be made efficient if the impediments faced by it are removed. The discussion on Strategic Trade Theory and Practice has brought out in sharp focus the strategic importance of "national interest" in any economic policy making. It has also emphasised the role of the State in conceptualing, identifying, formulating and the effectively implementing the policy-interventions. The invisible hand of the market and the visible hand of the State should together work in complete cohesion and harmony with the "national interest" as the prime objective.

What constitutes the "national interest" ? This is an important but a difficult question. I am reminded of the famous talisman given by Mahatma Gandhi. Gandhiji wrote way back in August 1947:

> "I will give you talisman. Whenever you are in doubt or when the self becomes too much with you, apply the following test. Recall the face of the poorest and the weakest man whom you have seen, and ask yourself if the step you contemplate is going to be of any use of him; Will he gain anything by it'. Will it restore him to a control over his own life and destiny? In other words, will it lead to Swaraj for the hungry and spiritually starving millions?"

This sums up the ideal philosophy of a national interest mode. In fact this given the basic framework for "fair" human bahaviour both at the national and at the international level. Of course practical interpretation of this philosophy for specific proper policy interventions, is a separate exercise in itself. The interpretations and their policy-corollaries could vary according to time stage, place and circumstances. But what is important is this talisman sets the "national interest" in the framework of a community welfare with the lowliest member of the community kept at the focus of analysis and that is eminently contrasts with the predatory "beggar-thy-neighbour" enshrined in the theory of strategic trade policy and brings human face to the imperatives of strategic policy responses. I strongly feel that this talisman could provide guiding principle for the reforms process in India.

There have been many national interest models for Indian development in the past. Dadabhai Naoroji's model based on Drain Theory, Mahatma Gandhi's model based on the principles of self-reliance and restraint on consumption, Babasaheb Ambedkar's model of social transformation and economic restructuring, Jawaharlal Nehru's model of industrialisation and technical change in a mixed economy framework, Rajiv Gandhi's model of modernisation and technological revolution,—to name only a few—are eminent examples of India's ingenuity in conceiving totally indigenous model of national interest. Each one of them is an optimal response to the national and global environment prevailing in the respective times taking into account the imperatives of the then relevant national aspirations. I consider it unfair if we criticise Nehruvian model, for instance, as a wrong choice by the criteria relevant for today's situation. The best of dynamic society lies in its ability to reform and readjust its national interest models to suit the changing economic environments. We are now set on the agenda of proving ourselves as an inherently dynamic society—of course without losing our foothold from the ground. The process of policy reform to rationalise the policy framework in India had started way back towards the end of the seventies......the famous Alexander Committee Report submitted in February 1978, had in a way laid the foundations of economic reforms of the external sector policies. This was of course supplemented by the recommendations of two other subsequent committees, viz., Tandon Committee and Abid Hussain Committee. But the reforms process had proceeded on a chequered path only to be revitalised and speeded up in the early nineties.

Is the problem of Level Playing Field (LPF) a real issue in the present context of liberalised trade regime ? I feel that it is an important issue which deserves sympathetic consideration and constant monitoring. Every exposure to competition should not be regarded as a case of LPF. However, the demand for LPF should not be interpreted to mean demand for protection of the kind that was available in the past. The demand for LPF becomes justified on several counts. Firstly, is the rationale of relative incentives. In regard to the incentives for the foreign investors and foreign suppliers of goods and services, relative to those offered to the domestic firms we may have the following alternative scenarios; (1) The relative concentives are just enough to attract the foreign firm to enter the domestic market and to offer to the domestic firm a fair competition; (2) The relative incentives are much more than what are just sufficient to attract the foreign from or (3) The relative incentives are less than sufficient. We presume that the last case is avoided. The second case would necessitate the LPF on the rationale that the profit earlier earned by the domestic firm is now transferred to the foreign firm on a platter, which may not be justified. One should carefully examine as to which of the above cases prevails in reality.

The second rationale comes from the fact that the reforms process has not yet percolated to the grass root level in the country, where the domestic firm has to operate. This is conveyed by the observation made in some quarters—may be jocularly made—that a local level officer now asks the domestic firm to bring the certificate from Delhi to the effect that no license is required, whereas earlier he was sending the firm to Delhi to bring license. Institutional and attitudinal revamping needed to give to the domestic economic actors the advantages of the reforms process has not been as yet completed. The third rationale arises from the strategic consideration that the foreign firm might already be the beneficiary of the policies of the foreign government, such as low interest rates, incentives for R & D, efficient mechanism for coverage of risks, good infrastructure etc.,—which provide to it undue or unfair advantage over the domestic firm. In short my argument is that the demand for LPF should be objectively examined on a case by case basis to remove the apparent anomalies in the process of evolving a competitive environment in the midst of imperfections of various kinds. I also urge that the domestic industry should not raise undue demands for LPF nor should it feel apologetic in asking for legitimate LPFs. There should be only pragmatism and not politics in this.

In order to monitor the process of structural adjustment and to identify the policy support measures required for strategic promotion of the targeted industries, multi-disciplinary commission on the lines of the Australian Industries Assistance Commission needs to be set up. This Indian Industries Assistance Commission (IIAC) should have academicians, industrialists and government officials on its Board. The main task of this commission is to hold public hearing on the "requirements" of the domestic industries—technological assistance, tariff protection, credit supplies, etc., and make recommendations for strategic policy interventions like the old Tariff Commission. Just as the Tariff Commission used to announce revenue-purpose tariffs and protective tariffs explicitly, it is useful to adopt this system once again. Protective tariffs and other strategic policy support measures should be transparent, time bound and their continuation of withdrawal in phases or at one go will have to be decided after the IIAC would have examined the current state of the domestic industry, its potential to become a strong export industry in the future etc. with public inquiry kind of analysis. This body should be totally technocratic and should be kept away from the domain of political or bureaucratic interference. It should be an advisory body but should have the status of a Commission to report directly to the Finance Minister. The aims and objects and the modalities of its functioning could be worked out on the same lines as the Australian Industries Assistance Commission, which is working very well in Australia.

Reduction in tariffs is one of the important components of the liberalisation process. With the complete elimination of the import licensing system, import tariffs are perhaps the only instruments of domestic protection. We can confess that import tariffs in India are perhaps higher than those in many other countries. That they should be reduced, cannot be contested. The analytical approach recommended in such situations, is to work out the tariff-reduction process in a phased manner. Firstly, equivalent tariffs will have to be worked out-equivalence in the sense that they provide the same level of protection and also production and trade effects, as was being accorded during the earlier licensing and tariff regime. In replacing the quota regime by the tariff regime, the first step is to impose these equivalent tariffs—of course with some upper ceilings. Even in this first phase itself, some tariffs could be less than the equivalent tariffs.

In the second phase, the equivalent tariffs would be reduced by a given time frame say 30% every year with a certain floor for each product category. The third phase should be a harmonised tariff regime in which spread across the sectors would be minimised but not necessarily eliminated. I believe that at any state of development, some sort differential tariff regime will have to be maintained in view of the technology-gap and various non-economic and "strategic interest" considerations. We may note that this was precisely the approach recommended in the Alexander Committee Report in 1978, and it is valid even today.

Another important aspect of this process of scaling downwards of the barriers should be done in a strategic reciprocation framework; What I have in mind is the following.

Right now, all countries are in the process of exchanging their schedules of offers for reciprocal concessions for trade, under GATT Round. I feel that the Finance Minister should not announce any radical tariff reductions in his budget but the Finance Ministry and the Commerce Ministry should together work out their strategic Policy responses to the ongoing process of the reciprocal offers being made under the Uruguay Round. Why should we feel apologetic and reduce our tariffs unilaterally when there is an opportunity to use them in the strategic game theoretic framework?

Export subsidies which had constituted a very great burden on the government's exchequer, have now been abolished -rightly so. Devaluation of the Rupee effected in 1991, 1992 and also in 1993, has provided an equivalent or even more than equivalent advantage to the export-sector. But there are three problems here. Surprisingly, rupee has shown tendencies of appreciation in recent mouths and the RBI has to buy dollars in huge quantum to avert and undue appreciation of the rupee. This approach can not continue too long. But of course with the prospects of increase in import-demand under the recovery process, demand for dollars would increase in the next few months. The tendency of appreciation would imply reduction in implicit export incentive and this should be checked. Secondly there are retaliatory devaluations in the other competing countries and thereby our relative competitive advantage would be reduced. Further, as it has happened in countries like Philippines and Malaysia, with increase in domestic inflation, the price-adjusted exchange rate may show more appreciation than depreciation. Thirdly, with increase in import cost export-production cost has also gone up. In agree that exchange rate is an effective tool for avoiding biases of one kind or the other. One will have to examine whether exchange rate manipulation alone could neutralise all the disadvantages which the domestic exporter faces in a competitive world market. Kindly forgive me, if I again go back to the Alexander Committee Report which had spelt out three criteria for rationalising the export-subsidy system. Export subsidies are required to neutralise the disadvantages faced by the domestic exporters, due to: (a) new markets and new products (b) unfair and discriminatory shipping costs and other freight rates and (c) the domestic fiscal and monetary policies covering high input taxes and interest rates. It was recommended that the first component should be phased out over a given time frame while the second and the third components need to be reviewed from time to time and adjusted.

It may be noted that the domestic exporters are interested in the net amount of rupees that they get ultimately for one dollar of export and hence the implicit exchange rate is more relevant than the official exchange rate. I am not sure whether somewhere in some Ministry, this kind of detailed analysis is done before coming to the conclusion, that devaluation has taken care of the export-incentive aspect of the policy. Further, as stated earlier, given the low scale of production and the very negligible low R &D intensity of production, domestic exporter has great structural disadvantages. The strategic policy response should be, as stated earlier, on of providing some incentives, support and facilities for expansion of scale and R & D activities. Does this not mean that currency devaluation may not be a sufficient measure for correcting the distortions in the product and factor markets? Should it not be supplemented by sector-targeted and purpose-targeted policy interventions?

Another area of strategic nature is one of export-services covering information, assistance for product-development and for technological upgradation, etc. It is a know fact of economic history that the JETRO—Japanese Export Trade Organisation, and KOTRA—Korean Trade Agency,—have played tremendous role in the export-revolution of these countries. Where is a similar export-service organisation in our country? Export-Promotion Councils, are not adequately equipped. Trade Development Authority and Trade Fair Authority together in their new incarnation as Indian Trade Promotion Organisation, and the National Trade Information Centre and Similar organisations are not yet geared up to the challenges set before them. All these institutions need to be strengthened and brought to the Centre stage of the export-promotion system. The state governments will have to set targets for export-expansion and not consider exports as Centre's responsibility.

International Trade Research and Teaching are one of the most strategic components of the infrastructure of trade promotion in the world over. Unfortunately we have not fully recognised this important element. Research in interrtational trade and international economic issues is ironically very much limited compared to research in other fields. Research infrastructure facilities, access to information and to current issues of policy relevance are all very limited. There is also the danger that the structural adjustment process—which has already put UGC and ICSSR under great resource constraints—would damage the research infrastructure, so eminently built up so far —beyond repaid. Competing countries would have extraordinary lead over us due to their superior research infrastructure for strategic trade policy making. I strongly feel that there should be concerted support for promoting international trade research and teaching.

I would like to flag one finaı thought on the strategic policy response of India, to the changing world economic scenario. I strongly feel that economics of neighbourhood is a great virtue for the South Asian region. Unfortunately, we have not taken full advantage of this natural virtue of the region. Of course, the real handicap is one of perception gaps and lack of mutual trust and respect. It is a peculiar kind of Prisoner's Dilemma situation—India apprehending that all other countries would "gang" up to isolate her and the other the countries fearing that India would dominate them. Both of these perceptions are misconceived and are based on inadequate appreciation of the potential benefits of cooperation and also sufficient awareness of the costs of non-cooperation. India should take leadership role—not in the big brother sense,—but as an effective and a benevolent patron of the region's progress. At the people-to-people level, there is tremendous desire to integrate and co-operate. We should make concerted efforts to intensity the process of intellectual dialogue among the social scientists, management consultants, technical experts, etc. We have made a small beginning in establishing a Network of the Economic Associations in the SAARC region. This Forum would further consolidate the various similar initiatives taken in the past for networking among researchers and research institutions.

Permit me to make another concrete proposal for taking full advantage of the economic neighbourhood. I strongly feel that we should declare some sub-regions of the South-Asian region as Rapid Economic Growth Belts (REGROBS)—cutting across the national borders. For example, Western, part of Bangladesh, eastern part of West Bengal in India, Bhutan and Tarai region of Nepal could be launched as a Growth-Trapezon or REGROB. Special development plans could be prepared and implemented in the framework of partnership in progress. Similarly, one could proclaim some sub-regions between India and Pakistan, and between India and Sri Lanka as REGROBS. Once the economic development gets the place of primacy in our mind-set, then many non-economic considerations would evaporated like mist under sun-rises. The evolution of such high growth belts would have significant spilt-over effects on the rest of the region. Some Indo-Pak joint ventures in production and trade and some Indo-Sri Lanka Joint-ventures aimed at inducing economic growth and employment creation, would eliminate over time, non-economic obsessions that pervade the politician's minds. The studies done by us in our Institution Research and Information System for the non-Aligned and other Developing Countries (RSI)—have identified many potential areas of joint ventures and trade for mutual benefits on the sub-regional basis. Thus, India's strategic policy response to the changing world economic scenario has various dimensions. Only one underlying principle is that of National interests.

CHAPTER 4

Railway Pricing and Finances in India

D.M. NANJUNDAPPA

INTRODUCTION

Indian Railways are the pride of the nation. With a route length of 62,462 Kms. with running track extending to 79,188 Kms. with nearly 22,000 Kms. of Electrified routes, 7,202 Locomotives, 3,527 Electric Multiple Unit Coaches, 36,000 Conventional Coaches, 3,15,000 Wagons and lifting 400 million tonnes of freight, 3,800 million passenger per year, Indian Railways is the largest railway network in the whole world. The total investment exceeds Rs. 32,000 Crores and they have employed 17 lakh workers, highest for any Public Sector Undertaking in India. They carry 1 crore passengers and 10 lakh tonnes of freight every day. Its management vests with the Railway Board consisting of 6 members and a Chairman, the former functioning as *Ex-officio* Secretaries to Government of India and he latter as *Ex-officio* Cabinet Secretary. They have contributed to national integration and have promoted the development of backward areas by enabling opening up of natural resources in different regions of the country through the railway network. Obviously, such a big and complex system would call for massive resources for its operation. Its total gross revenue exceeds Rs. 18,000 crores per year and the cost exceed Rs. 16,500 crores. Indian Railways are the only standing example in the whole world of earning profits, especially over the past 6-8 years continuously. Its pricing and finance are, therefore, of crucial significance to both the development and management of the Indian economy.

STRUCTURE OF RAILWAY BUDGET

Railway have a budget of their own into which all earnings are credited and from which all expenditures are met. On the receipts side, in addition, they show the budgetary support given by the Government of India, through their General budget. Due to inadequacy of budgetary resources, the railways are also given non-budgetary support in the form of loans raised from the Market through the Indian Railway Financial Corporation (IRFC). These are taken to credit on the receipt side and the corresponding interest and loan repayment is shown on the expenditure side. They also set aside a substantial amount for the Depreciation Reserve Fund, and transfer certain funds to the Revenue Reserve Fund, Development Fund, Pension Fund, Accident, Compensation Safety and Passenger Maintenance Fund and these are reflected in their budget. The railways can easily draw on all these funds except the Depreciation Reserve Fund in which case, while withdrawals are generally permitted for repairs and maintenance, funds from it cannot be utilised for investment in so far as the Central Government teats the idle funds as a part of the national kitty. All payments and the dividends from the railways on the capital at charge are debited to the expenditure account. In the year of losses they are met by the General Budget. Therefore, the position of the railway users can be easily generalised under this system as it boils down to one of railway costs—railway user payments relationship. This is unlike the roads system, where such generalisation becomes very difficult.

The railways follow a system of fully distributed costs in

arriving at the unit costs of their major activities. The costing done faces severe limitations. When railway user payments are not rationally linked in costs, total payments may be either higher or lower than the total railway supply costs. The predicament of the Indian Railway users, as alleged that fare and freight charges are high and that they are being hiked too often in recent years without showing improvements in the quality of service or reduction in their supply costs, is explained by not scientifically relating all the user payments to the costs. Reasons for the disadvantageous resources position of railways are many. The most important is that they are looked upon as public utility although the policy as per the Indian Railway Act is one of reiterating the need for railways to function as commercial enterprises. Due to this confused interpretation, populist measures of charging the railway users too much below the cost in respect of passengers and commuters and in the case of certain commodities like foodgrains, salt, sugarcane, fodder, fertilisers, fruit, and vegetables, marble, other ores, etc., are followed. Consequently, the losses incurred on this account and from the operation of uneconomic lines are mounting each year.[1] The pricing policy presently followed is based on the principles of cost of service and the value of service and find resources for cross subsidisation from the surplus on freight traffic. The pressure for resources for financing Five Year Plans and the feeling of the Planners that cheaper railway transport services are to be provided for promoting faster growth has led to either incurring of heavy losses or generating marginal surpluses that are too inadequate to finance railway development, both its network expansion and modernisation. In addition, there is a reluctance to spend adequate amounts on proper maintenance of the railway assets including track, coaches, wagons and locomotives, perhaps due to the resource crunch. A major explanation is that railways are considered as social over-heads, the provision of which is the responsibility of the Government and are not allowed to function as commercial enterprises. It must be noted that railway services are sold to the public and therefore they can utilise consumer preference or choice to attract the funds required to meet the users demand. If the revenue raised from rail user charges until now were found inadequate for investment in railways, it was for the reason that they found in the railway budget a convenient means to finance budgetary deficits by starving the railways of funds. Under the New Economic Policy, the railways are told that if they raised more of their internal resources, they can have a larger Investment Plan. With this, the accent is more on the proper pricing of the railway services for achieving efficient resources allocation and optimal development of the railway network as well as railway transport as a core infrastructure industry.

A pricing system serves the dual function of: (a) distributing a given quantity of railway services in such a way as to serve the greatest need and (b) supplying the right quantity of railway services and producing them in the most efficient manner. Its application to railways is rendered difficult because railways, unlike some other industries, have very large common costs (joint cost) which are very difficult to distribute in any system of pricing on the basis of marginal cost, which refers to the quantum of real sources asked for providing an extra unit of railway service. Therefore, considerable adaptation is needed to accommodate the distinguishing characteristics like that of joint costs as well as the different roles which the Government, as the owner of the monopoly, would like to pursue.

Certain characteristics of railways are of great relevance to their pricing.

(1) Lumpy Investment and Creation of High Capacity in Advance

Once a railway is built it can have no other function but to provide services along its route. It cannot be stored and excess capacity in any one segment cannot be made available at any other place at a time. thus, unutilised capacity has not alternative use in the short run and its economic value is zero.

(2) Joint Cost and the Bye-Product Nature of Railway Services

On the same railway track, different types of trains run and in the railway workshops heterogeneous products are manufactured for use in assets like the rails, coaches, wagons, locomotives, etc., It has more capacity for capacity for carrying traffic and at greater speed.

(3) Decreasing cost with longer Distance and Successive Block of Output

The railways share with other large-scale undertakings, economies of scale. Excess capacity may be obtaining in some segments and congestion in others which create problems for pricing. A special feature is the invisibility or lumpiness attendant on long-run or intermediate run costs for a smaller size of the railway plant that is technically feasible. The other is the long-run decreasing costs with indivisabilities or without them depending on discontinuties or possibilities of continuous modifications in the process of achieving long-run economies of scale. If the growth is slow or if high interest rates increase the cost of building ahead of demand, indivisibility may take on a life of its own as a source of pricing difficulties.

(4) Continuity of Capital Stock

The railway network, in a sense, can never be completely replaced. To meet additional demand it is only necessary to add to or modify the existing capital stock. The track, if property maintained, can be a long lasting asset. This creates conceptual difficulties for defining costs.

As a vast enterprise of the Government, if railways are required to function like commercial enterprises, they have to conform to such economic and commercial obligations as are common to all commercial enterprises in the public sector. A price policy which is appropriate for railways must be determined in the context of the following guidelines:

(a) Pricing of railway services should be such as to yield a net return that corresponds to the scarcity value of the capital in the economy;
(b) The price charged for the railway facility must have a close relationship to the costs of providing it;
(c) Monopoly pricing is to be avoided as it is considered

to be against public interest for reasons that are well-known.

The case for determining railway user charges thus centres on the feasibility and desirability of adopting full cost or marginal cost as the basis of charging for the railway service.

FULL COST PRICING

Under full cost pricing, total costs of the railways should be divided among users charging individual users the costs incurred on their behalf for providing the service. Where the costs differ from one railway to another, payments should in principle be related to individual railways; but, in practice, they are related to costs of the railway system as a whole.

Full cost pricing operates the average cost charging mechanism through a single or a two-part tariff. Under both the methods, users are subjected to uniform rates; but, the two-part tariff comprises a fixed and a variable levy while the two portions are blended into one part under the single part tariff.

If there is to be no waste or resources, the pricing principle should be to restrain journeys or traffic when they are valued at less than the costs or losses railway users cause to other sand encourage journeys when they are valued at more than the costs they cause. This means that the price should equal the costs of wear and tear, on the railways and congestion costs. For uncongested railway only the costs of wear and tear are to be recovered. The average cost pricing leads to inefficient resource allocation as it ignores the optimising rule. Users of uncogested railways are overcharged and those of congested routes undercharged, resulting in limitless demand for railways in congested areas which cannot be easily met. Thus, it does not provide any guideline for deciding investment in railways.

When railway services are provided at prices below their cost, there arises a conflict between the interests of the individual in his capacity as the user and in his capacity as a provider of the service (tax payer under the system of railways being financed from the General Budget).

When the same price is charged for all users irrespective of the quantum of the facility used and the costs incurred on their behalf, it is bound to be inequitable. The extent to which a fairer distribution of the cost can be achieved depends on identifying the costs with respect to each user. But, this difficulty arises under any pricing system in so far as joint costs are involved in the provision of railway services.

A major criticism is that average cost doctrine says nothing about what charges should be levied as what matters to it is total revenue. This may not be a serious limitation, because the defect lies not in the doctrine but in the choice of charges. Given the constraint of cost recovery, the charges can be chosen keeping in view their relation to railway use. By increasing the rates of charges that are closely related to railway asset use and by reducing the rates of those that are remotely connected with railway use, a rate-mix that brings a revenue equal to costs can be decided.

Under the two-part tariff, a railway user will pay a variable charge equal to the marginal cost of his use and a fixed charge to reflect the benefit he derives from the facility (fixed costs). It has some similarity with perfect discrimination and its optimality depends closely on the extent to which the fixed charge approaches the surplus to each consumer who uses the railway. Since the fixed charge is generally identical for all users, some will enjoy a surplus over and above the fixed charge and others who would have used the railway if they had to pay only the variable charge would be excluded from using it. Thus, unless the fixed charge[2] can be made to equal each individual consumer's surplus, a two-part tariff seems to be little better than average cost pricing.

Full cost ensures by any of the two applications that only those who benefit from the railway pay for its use, but exclude those who would use it at marginal cost. It provides an ex-post check on investment. Where a railway project has benefits greater than costs but costs cannot be recovered in charges, the project will have to be given up and this may result in a dead-weight loss to society.

In so far as demand is distributed between roads and railways at prices that reflect the relative costs of providing different services, the overall profitability of each mode of transport will reflect more adequately the extent to which that mode of transport is able to maximise social benefits or minimise social cost. In this sense and on the assumption of the no divergence between costs and social costs on the one hand and consumers' preference as expressed in the market and social benefits on the other hand, profitability of railway under full cost pricing can serve as indicator for future investment decision.

MARGINAL COST PRICING

Under the Marginal Cost approach, the price to be charged for railway service should be equal to only additional costs generated by one more unit of railway service. The basis of charging is the value of resources consumed by an additional user. A price which is equal to the real economic costs of using the railway services brings about an optimal allocation of resources. Such a price ensures that railway output would be expanded to the point and only to the point at which the cost of producing an additional unit of railway services would equal the price that users would be prepared to pay for it. In the familiar price theory jargon, it means a price equal to marginal cost.

A firm's costs are a function not only of the rate of output per period, but also of the number of periods during which production takes place, the total volume of production and the period when output starts. So, there need not be only one marginal cost. Similarly, in railways, depending on whether the adjustment is meant for a quick or permanent increase in output, two marginal cost concepts are involved.

1. Short Run Marginal Cost (S.R.M.C.); and
2. Long Run Marginal Cost (L.R.M.C.).

S.R.M.C. pricing rule suggests that in view of the spatial and temporal fixity of the railway track and other assets, price should equal only those costs which are immediately responsive to changes in the level of output. This means a price equal to variable maintenance cost (i.e., operating costs, wear and tear of the track and rolling stock and if congestion prevails, the cost imposed on other users (i.e., congestion costs). Since capital invested in railways cannot be switched to other users easily, capital costs are not to be included in the charge.

S.R.M.C. pricing is advocated for two reasons. First, as the proportion of annual capital cost to variable maintenance cost is high, the difference between full cost and S.R.M.C. will be considerable and consequently in principle, it has a potential for greater efficiency. Secondly, capital costs are incurred in frequently because of the long physical life of railway assets. This implies long periods during which the main problem is one of getting the best use of existing resources and this is best achieved by S.R.M.C. pricing. The second reason has to be played down considerably in the case of a country like India where the maintenance of its assets leaves much to be desired.

L.R.M.C. includes all costs, fixed as well as variable maintenance costs, associated with the production of an extra unit of railway facility. There are difficulties of determining the L.R.M.C. in the case of railways due to their characteristics, especially (1) and (4) discussed earlier. As a way of getting cut of these difficulties, the method of treating capital expenditure in a given year as a current item was suggested and adopted by the U.K. Transport Ministry.[3] If this is accepted, L.R.M.C. pricing means price equal to capital costs in any given year plus the variable maintenance costs in that year per unit of output. This cannot be accepted since it conflicts directly with the notion of capital investment in any venture. Moreover, Turvey has shown that neither provision for obsolescence for depreciation calculated on a replacement basis directly enter into marginal cost and any attempt to set prices on such a basis is incompatible with marginal cost pricing.[4] It may also be noted that when in equilibrium, S.R.M.C. and L.R.M.C., are equal and then need be no reduction in output.[5]

Two major issues emerge from these two pricing doctrines: (1) loss of output under average cost pricing, and (2) emergence of deficits under marginal cost (S.R.M.C. or L.R.M.C.) pricing which has consequences for investment funds and distribution of income.

As the condition Price equals Marginal Cost ensures optimal output, it is argued that the deficit must be covered by subsidies if the capital stock is to be renewed and such a policy is preferable to the alternative of setting the price sufficiently high to cover its costs. For, this would place society on a lower level of satisfaction than if the railway facility were priced at marginal cost and losses covered through taxation.

The objections to marginal cost (S.R.M.C. or L.R.M.C.) pricing are by now well known. We simply list them here for completeness and comment later about what can be the appropriate pricing policy for Indian Railways. The objections are:

1. Earnings will be inadequate to meet the costs and there will be uncertainty about deficits being covered;
2. The resulting distribution of benefits will be contrary to equity consideration;
3. Some costs are imposed on third parties and those who bear these costs may not be able to collect them; similarly some benefits may be conferred on third parties who cannot be made to contribute to the cost;
4. It is difficult to identify the costs of different services and where unpredictability obtains in the need of a service resulting in higher costs, some form of average cost pricing may become necessary;
5. Marginal costs are not charged in the rest of the economy or in competing services like the roads; and
6. It is not easy to say whether railway services are produced under decreasing, increasing or constant costs.

CHOICE OF PRICE POLICY

Before proceeding to examine whether average or marginal cost pricing (S.R.M.C. or L.R.M.C.) is desirable for Indian Railways, we should note that the choice must be relevant to goals of policy and institutional framework to which it applies.

Different forms of pricing lead to varying patterns of resource utilisation. A price policy that is considered appropriate for a given objective turns out to be inappropriate when goals of policy differ. In general, pricing considerations relevant to the Indian rural sector and backward areas will not be relevant to the urban and developed sector.

The aims of Indian economic policy can be put into the following broad categories;

1. Promote optimal investment and higher growth of the economy.
2. Achieve improvements in quality and productivity through encouraging competition;
3. Encourage exports to solve the balance of payments problem;
4. Mobilise resources for financing development especially the core sectors like Agriculture, Rural Development, Health, Power and other basic infrastructure;
5. Integration of Indian Economy with the global markets; and
6. Eliminate all obstacles to free entry and inflow of capital by deregulation and privatisation.

In principle, these aims need not conflict with one another but in practice it is more likely that any one of hem gets pushed only at the expense of the other due to the difficulties of reconciling to a combination of all which is acceptable as appropriate.

With continued deficits, the railways will not have enough

internal resources and with possibilities of getting budgetary support being 'Nil' and the private investment shying away due to losses affects severely the growth of the economy. In fact, capital attraction to investment in railways depends upon the availability of grants from the public exchequer to meet the deficit. In the existing circumstances when revenue and fiscal deficits are mounting, optimal investment appears to be a mirage.

As the railway transport cost forms a very insignificant part of the total manufacturing costs, to attempt achieving larger exports by offering lower freight charges is uncertain to generate better performance in exports. Experience reveals that the railway freight structure included incentives for bulk items like iron ore has not led to much of the desired results. A better edge should be found in producing quality products at internationally competitive prices or using iron ore in the country itself for export of manufactured iron and steel of high quality.

More resource mobilisation is constrained by increasing non-plan expenditure and lack of a fair return on investment in public sector projects. In so far, as resource crunch is confronting almost all sectors, pricing policy of the railways should aim at generating more surpluses without sacrificing the quality of service. Instead marginal surpluses or negative surpluses and dependence on budgetary support worsen the country's revenue and fiscal deficits resulting in strong inflationary pressures.

Competition is meaningful as an end when the rules of the game obtain alround. In an imperfect market system, railways alone adopting the marginal cost pricing conductive for competition cannot assure improvements in quality of service or its productivity. In fact, with deficits glaring in the very eyes, even marginal investment needs for quality improvement and higher productivity become elusive.

Globalisation focuses on faster industralisation taking advantage of the international division of labour and the markets for the domestic economy. This cannot be the exclusive privilege or concern of the railways alone. While efficient railway transport can only contribute to timely movement of goods and people, it can seldom achieve integration all by itself. It is unlikely that the Indian Railways can play any major direct role in this matter.

The last objective of free entry/inflow of foreign capital is a non-pricing issues. Fiscal controls and licencing need to be removed for foreign capital to come to any area open to it. Administered prices frighten away new entrants as well as capital. While railways still are subject to some type of administered price or the other, no special advantage can be claimed. On the side of privatisation, the massive or lumpy investments with long gestation periods, seem to be far beyond the reach of the private sector. More than this only activities which are highly profitable can attract private capital, either domestic or international. This also falls into non-price phenomena, in the sense that a decision to throw open investment in profitable segments of the Indian Railways for participation by private capital does not automatically bring into the country the surplus capital elsewhere. A decidedly decisive decision in parceling out certain activities to the private needs to be taken. Even so, political and social unrest in the country can frighten away intending investors.

We will now briefly examine what form of pricing can be considered most suitable for Indian Railways.

OPTIMUM ALLOCATION AND GROWTH

The assumption behind marginal cost pricing that all goods are sold at marginal cost and all factor receive their marginal product throughout the economy is negative in most of the countries due to taxes, externalities and monopoly conditions of some degree or other. When this is so, charging marginal cost for the railway service leads to its over utilisation and the value of the marginal factor employment in the railways will be less than its value in other sectors. Consequently, national income can be increased by shifting resources out of the railway sector. This suggests the possibility of second best solutions, and the desirability and wisdom of adjusting the prices and/or costs of public enterprises on to shadow prices in developing countries is not all that clear.

It is noticed that price is not the only determining factor in the shift of traffic. Partly due to the policy of railways namely, preference to the long distance rake load traffic over the short distance and the smalls' traffic, traffic has shifted considerably, especially freight to the roads. Yet another reason is the poor quality of service and the lack of door to door delivery in case of railways. It is also observed that contrary to popular belief that beyond 500 Kms. upto which road transport is said to have advantageous, bulk traffic is carried by road notwithstanding even the higher prices perhaps due to assured timely delivery, no pilferage, and spot delivery. There is a special feature namely, even when the road charge relatively a low price when compared to railways, they try to make up for the difference and even earn more by accepting traffic on the return trip. To the extent that the railways wish to regain their traffic lost to the roads, the price may have to move towards the marginal cost rather than the average cost in which case railways incur huge deficits. Moreover, even assuming that marginal cost pricing will lead to optimal development of railways, in reality, the resources of that order are not available for the railways to develop their network so as to cope-up with the optimal demand.

CHARGING PRINCIPLE IN COMPETING SERVICES

It is important that at least the roads, the main competitor to railways should be observing the marginal cost rule, if the same is to be adopted by railways. Otherside, maximum benefits cannot be achieved and problems of transport co-ordination will have to be encountered.

In so far as the Indian Railways are charging a price which is less than marginal cost for some commodities and practice price discrimination due to the constraint on total costs, more traffic is attracted to railways because of lower than marginal cost and consequently the major contributing factor for railway deficits does not shift. The result is over utilisation in certain routes and idle capacity in some others have developed on the railways.

When Marginal Cost Pricing is not followed by the

competitor like roads, asking the railways to adopt marginal cost pricing is arguing in a circle and is only another way of commanding the rest of the economy to adopt it. The road users in India pay more than the total costs of road provision.[7] Thus, when cost plus pricing prevails in the road sector, the change sought is one of the transition from it to marginal cost pricing whereas in respect of railways, it is one movement from below marginal cost and average cost plus pricing towards marginal cost pricing.

If price is made equal to marginal cost in both the railways and roads, there would not doubt be an efficient allocation between railways and roads, but there would be overutilisation of transport services in relation to other sectors of the economy where average cost plus pricing trends to prevail. When railways price some competitive goods at rates substantially in excess of their marginal cost, pricing the roads at marginal costs, aggravates the under utilisation of railways. Adopting S.R.M.C. pricing in both means deficits on both accounts. Thus, it becomes impracticable and politically and financially unacceptable.

Moreover, deliberate introduction of marginal cost pricing in the public policy can be achieved only over a period of time and when the economy is poised for getting the maximum output from the existing rail facilities and is not concerned with investing more in their expansion to open up rural areas. In this direction as approximation to average cost pricing for both roads and railways as a first step seems to be a smooth and feasible transition. The rise in price of railways fro below marginal cost to average cost will help eliminate deficits and there will be some loss of benefits caused by the stopping of the shift of traffic to less efficient mode of transport from a more efficient one. It should be reiterated that any particular form of pricing cannot be advocated for railways ignoring what prevails in the competing modes of transport.

SATURATED Vs. IDLE CAPACITY ROUTES

Congestion costs are central to the theme of S.R.M.C. pricing. Price must equal congestion cost and variable maintenance and operating costs. Only the golden quadrilateral connecting the four Metropolitan cities and its diagonal are congested (carrying traffic at saturated points and beyond) and other similar urban routes have congestion costs. On other including the rural sectors, there is high idle capacity. Hence, by definition congestion costs are zero. The rail user charges are therefore to equal congestion costs and variable costs on saturated routes while on non-saturated routes with idle capacity, only the variable cost has to be met. Such a policy encourages greater use of less utilised routes and discourages traffic in congested parts if the journey is valued at less utilised routes and discourages traffic in congested parts if the journey is valued at less than the costs they impose on others. Such a charging principle will bring about optimal utilisation of all routes. It is possible that some surplus revenue may be generated on the highly saturated routes which may be set to some extent the losses on high idle capacity routes. This recipe raises two issues. One is connected with the fairness of a price that is equal to variable maintenance costs for idle capacity routes, if the maintenance costs in such routes is lesser than that on saturated routes. The second, which is intertwined with the first relates to the possibility of covering the deficit.

Pricing the idle capacity and uneconomic routes at zero marginal costs may appear to those who feel that cheaper or free transport will stimulate development of backward areas. By similar logic, a higher price is to be charged to equal congestion and variable costs on the highly saturated rates. It would be unfair to make the congested rail route user pay congestion costs at a level of congestion to which he is not mainly possible. They are more due to the basic deficiencies of the railway network rather than to the increased traffic flow.

Charging on zero marginal costs leads to still greater deficits that whittle down the development of railways.[8]

A desirable solution seems to lie in emphasising both total and marginal cost.

INVESTMENT SIGNALS

Unlike the roads, where the problem of investment gets distributed over the supplier of the road track and the users of the road track, in railways, investment for railway track and rolling stock, terminals, signaling equipment, workshops, production units, etc., is thrust on one and same agency, the Railway Ministry. Where new railway lines are laid, investment for infrastructure to generate traffic in the catchment area falls on the State Governments and the rest depends on the location of firms. Can pricing railway services provide the required signals for such investment decisions?

Investment decision are to be based on expected benefits over estimated costs. Inadequate maintenance expenditure in the past or improving an existing railway cannot automatically command a priority on resources. Whether they must have a first claims on resources prior to further construction of new railway lines should be decided only after an analysis of comparative benefits to be derived from the same resources devoted to another alternative investment. There is a strong bias for constructing new lines, gauge conversion, introducing new trains, etc., rather than properly maintaining the existing assets.

Another aspect is related to the decision on initial capital investment. In so far as investment funds are to come from the general budget (the tax payer in the country) there will arise the relative priorities of competing demand of other sectors. Strictly speaking, the opportunity costs of such capital should enter the decision making process. Yet another relevant point is the need to maintain inter-sectorial balances between an infrastructure industry like the railway transport and production and service sectors of the domestic economy. To the extent that the railway user charges are either at marginal costs or below the marginal cost, generation of internal resources by way of surplus for investment in railways will be negative. Perhaps one may ask the question: Can the need for heavy initial investment be reduced by phased development of the railway network? This may apply for shorter platforms even where longer rakes are operating single track where double track is required, continue with the existing gauge (metre or narrow) than going in for massive gauge conversion programme to achieve the objective of uni-gauge system, may temporarily reduce the demand for capital funds. A special feature of the railways that must be kept in view is that due to heavy investment required and the long gestation period, railways ought to be built to a higher capacity. The argument that the shortages in themselves bring about the pressure for the supply of investment for the expansion of the railway network can lead to a low level of output and satisfaction which may or may not be conducive for the growth of the India economy. The final answer depends on anticipated levels of traffic on railway sand operative costs and benefits of developing railways to alternative higher levels of capacity and specifications. It is also to be reckoned that the planning costs under phased construction may by no means be low. On the contrary the absolute total needed for railways under phased construction can invariably be greater that if it is unphased. Mistakes and dangers and costly errors are likely in such programmes. Therefore this calls for great care in their formulation. Pricing of any form does not provide all the full information required for this decision.

It has been argued that the emergence of the surpluses and the deficit under SRMC pricing on a given segment of the railway network would give the signal for expansion of contraction of investment. Those parts of the system on which revenues exceed outgoings should expand until the surplus disappears; those on which the outgoing exceed revenues should contract or atleast not expand unless uses are prepared to pay the costs of railways use or unless the government subsidies such segments.

This principle supposes that the different segments are independent and decision making is fully decentralised. Also it supposes the practicability of maintaining separate costs and receipts for each segment of the railway network. The implications of this are the uneconomic/rural sector where deficits are perennial would continue to face the threat of contraction of closing down or atleast no hope of expansion although the need of that area and the people may be the greatest.

If finance is to come from the general budget as a whole, should be there be additional taxation on all or on only those who benefit from the railway facility? Why should not the better off segment of the railway system subsidise the weak segments? For instance, the freight which his comparatively in the better off segments may subsidise the passengers travelling n the second class ordinary. There is also no certainty like the mass transit system will not show up deficiencies. These are the type of consequences that follow and they do not provide information which only the cost-benefit approach can give for investment decisions.

In so far as transport costs from a small faction of the total manufacture costs, expecting in an item like coal, the leverage available for manipulating output through the reduction in the rail user charges may be very little. But from the view-point of financing investment, what price is charged for the railway use matters considerably as the difference between the average cost and the marginal cost of providing the railway facility is large.

With investment also tied upto other decision to locate the firms, there are two issues in this reckoning. (1) less than full cost pricing may lead to inefficient allocation (2) marginal cost pricing may attract industries to less developed areas. Firms may take wrong location decisions, and make the government build the railways so that their uneconomic project may become justified. SRMC pricing may make the government react in this way only in respect of already take decisions when making use of the cost benefit approach and it is unlikely that any firm will add to existing risks of making the location decision the risks involved in getting government action. If marginal costs pricing is adopted the real resources cost of using the railway will be automatically included in the firm's decision and any rent associated with the location will appear as a cost differential in such a decision irrespective of who gets the rent. The defence based on uncertainly hanging over the prospects of making the government take wrong decisions is rather weak. There is increased evidence to show that foot loose industries come up in many areas that have no locational specific advantages.

Therefore, the inducement of low transport costs must be accepted with a little caution. Other incentives seem to play a very decisive role in location decisions. The Government policy has to be more oriented towards providing other infrastructure like roads, markets, banking, power supply, housing, water, etc., in the catchment area of the railway lines. In is thus the government that moves first expecting the industry to follow. There is also enough evidence to show that decisions are taken to locate public sector undertakings in less developed areas as a measure of spreading growth. As to how private firms react to the construction of a railway line, it is difficult to give a definite answer. It all depends on the benefit from the railway as a proportion of the package benefit offered to attract the firms to a given area. Where the later dominates, it is more likely as benefits from reduced transport costs constitute a very small fraction of the total benefits, charging the full costs for the railway service may not be a disincentive. Secondly, the case for adopting marginal cost pricing as an incentive to attract firms to less developed or rural areas becomes very weak.

RESOURCE MOBILISATION: INTERNATIONAL SURPLUSES

There can be several reasons for building up international surplus in the Railway Budget.

Firstly, railways are to pay the dividend of 6.5% on the total Capital at-charge which is given to them as a loan in perpetuity. This represents the interest on the loan given to the Railways. In the event of no surplus or inadequate surplus the dividend liability gets deferred to that extent and will have to be paid in the year when larger surpluses accrue to the railways. In the meanwhile, the deficit in the general budget goes up to that extent and it has to be met by the general budget.

Secondly, in the New Economic Policy, railways are required to function more as commercial enterprises in which case the dependence on the general budget for both revenue and development needs is either reduced or eliminated. Particularly in the budget of the Railways of 1996-97, the budgetary support is only Rs. 1269 crores or 15.6%. The Balance 84.4% of the total out-lay each year will have to be generated by the railways as surplus from their internal resources. In fact, the future development of the railway network, modernisation and providing adequate and efficient railway transport depends upon the size of the surplus. In the event of the losses the railway will be compelled not only to reduce their development but also to seek loans from the Government for meeting the losses.

Thirdly, the transport cost in manufacturing forms a negligible proportion except in the case of low value commodity like coal or bulk commodity like iron and steel, cement, etc. The transport cost as such is spread over large output catering to the consumers throughout the length and breadth of the country. Where there are exports making use of the railway transport, the incidence of freight falls on the foreign consumers. Therefore generating surplus, poses no threat of stimulating inflationary pressure in the country.

Fourthly, from the point of equity, the railways can adopt discriminating monopoly prices for upper class passengers like AC I Class, I Class, AC II Class and Sleeper Class. They can be made to pay a higher fare leading to a surplus which can cross subsidise the lower fare charged for the II Class ordinary passengers. There will be some kind of income redistribution about which more will be said later on.

Fifthly, the contribution to the general budget made by the railway earnings will finance the development in other sectors. In this way, benefits of overall growth come back to the Railways in the form of increased demand for railway transport. Thus, there will be a feedback and the surplus is a payment for the amounts that accrue to the railway users from development.

Finally, the direct relationship of offering of the railway service and the benefit of travel/traffic to users, unlike the taxes which are not *quid-pro-quo* payments renders the railway fare and freight for the services. Surpluses may have repercussions on the demand as well as on tolerance of the general public especially the computers. But in so far as the benefit is conferred, payment covering the cost of the service need not be less attractive.

The charging principle based on the benefit criteria invariably becomes an instrument of recovering the cost of the benefit. Transport is in a large measure an intermediate good and a very steep hike in fare and freight can have repercussions for efficiency in the production of wide range of outputs. Reliance on railway user payments to create surplus should not be at the cost of diversion of traffic and more distortions in the economy.

REDISTRIBUTIVE FUNCTION

Income redistribution is not a direct objective of the new economic policy, which aims at a higher growth rate. Reduction in income inequality is to be achieved indirectly through higher growth of the Indian economy. Therefore, Railway pricing is not to be assessed from the view point of achieving income redistribution.

The level of inequality and its changing pattern has raised some issues. The degree of concentration of wealth and overall income inequality has somewhat increased in the urban sector. Distribution of income in the rural sector is also becoming less equal. Again distribution varies among different occupational classes like salaried employees, self-employed and the owners of property. Available data show that contractors among the self-employed have greatly improved their position and those engaged in transport manufacturing and financial policies are also fairly well off.

Changes in the method of railway pricing inevitably cause changes in the distribution of income. Some people gain more than others when the charge is below the cost of service while some people will lose. The way in which the pricing affects the different sectors of occupational classes depends on the manner in which the earnings from the pricing system are used by the Railways. In the present pricing system, where the intentional surplus is very marginal, there is a transfer of income from freight customers to passenger customers. Not all railway users can be said to be well-off. In the case of industrialists and businessman who are the railway users, the incidence of higher pricing will not rest on the richer class because they may be shifted on to the consumers of the goods produced or sold. In the cases of passengers and commuters whose travelling expenditure is not met either by their employers or from sources other than their income (salary) the incidence will rest with them. While this may not lead to any pressure on inflation, shifting of higher railway price in the case of freight can be inflationary. But it is difficult to say what actually is the distribution affect in the case of non-railway users. In the case of the raising of the freight on items food-grains, fertilisers, etc., the effect on distribution of income will be marked in the case of poor farmers within the agricultural sectors. As contractors and those engaged in business and industry make use of railways to a greater extent than other in carrying out their work. The railways getting higher revenue from the better-off sections may be a welcome effect but one cannot be sure that among the non-railway users, benefits have accrued to only those who are in the low income groups. Equally uncertain is the presumption that contractors have not shifted the burden on the railway user charges.

Intentional surpluses are to be achieved in the railway budget not as a fleeting feature. The surplus in the railway budget has two cosequences; one is that under marginal cost pricing and the deficit that has arisen will have to be wiped out and investiable funds become available to the railway for investment. The other aspect is the relation of the surplus to the general budget. With a reduction in the budgetary support to the railways, the overall budget deficit has been reduced. In fact, in 1995-96, the budgetary deficit of the Government of India was Rs. 7600 crores. This deficit would have been more, by Rs. 1583 crores had the railways not paid the dividend (Rs. 1583 crores) on the capital-at-charge in that year. Any increase in the surplus would make available internal resources for the Railway Investment Plan. The point that is to be emphasised is that the influence of the larger surplus on the general budget would be in the form of assisting the Government of India in reducing both its revenue deficit and the fiscal deficit, and at the same time enable the railways to maintain a rate of growth which can sustain a higher growth rate of the Indian economy. Why should railway users be made to pay higher charges for leaving a large surplus of a pre-determined size[9] like say Rs. 5000? This would not be used for financing any general expendiutre or the rising cost from which they did not derive any additional traffic benefit. In so far as the surplus is earmarked for the railway development and not for any non-developmental expenditure, it should be a welcome feature. Otherwise, there will be only disbenefits to share.

Such a surplus needs recovery of total cost and generating a return of about 16% on capital invested. It may be argued that instead of fixing the fares and frieght on the cost plus fair return basis, the deficit that may arise from marginal cost pricing can be covered from certain other sources of finance which are within the realm of railways. In particular, land and other property values going up as result of railway development can be considered for the levy of development charge. It is perfectly reasonable to argue that land that benefits from a railway line must contribute towards the cost of construction and the revenue raised from some form of texation on land, whatever the yield, could add to funds available for railway development. However, it is not far from truth if it is concluded that under the present circumstances, it would be utopian to expect revenue from such levies would be adequate to meet the deficit in the railway budget arising from S.R.M.C. Pricing.

In assessing the effects of pricing on the deficits, another important factor to be taken into account is the general economic situation in the Indian Economy. Normally if aggregate demand is less than the full employment level, it needs to be stepped up and allowing a deficit to develop or increase in such a situation is not per se bad. But the Indian economy has been experiencing strident inflation and lacks complementary resources which are required to offset the effects of increased spending. In such a context, any increase in deficit implies a further inflationary stimulus which is just what should not be allowed to happen. In so-far as S.R.M.C. pricing or L.R.M.C. pricing enhance the railway budgetary deficit and through the overall budgetary deficit of the Government of India, it will only contribute to further instability. The increase in overall deficit will be less under average cost pricing. In one case, loss from increased deficits are to be balanced against the gains in efficient resource allocation; in the other, gains from freight-reduced deficits are to be balanced against losses from inefficient resource allocation.

FACTUAL APPLICATION

In the following, we try to illustrate the consequence of alternative pricing policies of the railway with reference to over-all budgetary position of 1993-94.

RAILWAY BUDGET UNDER MARGINAL COST

(S.R.M.C. and L.R.M.C.) and Average Cost Pricing in Relation to Over-all Railway Budgetary Position 1993-94

Rs. in crores

A.	**Revenue and Cost**		
	Railway Gross Revenue		17946.02
	Total Railway Costs (Ordinary working expenses + DRF + Pension Fund + Payment of Dividend)		16430.59
	Short run marginal costs (SRMC) (Ordinary working expenses + Payment of dividend) (interest on capital)		13055.59
B.	**Deficit (-) or Surplus (+) in Railway Budget**		
	Under S.R.M.C. Pricing	-	3375.00
	Under average cost pricing	+	1515.43
	Under L.R.M.C. Pricing (Ordinary working expenses + interest on capital (dividend) + investment in 1992-93)	-	1618.01
C.	**Contribution of Railway Budget to Overall Budgetary Position in the Country**		
	As per the system of railway accounts		

	presently followed by the Railway Ministry (Railway Board) Dividend + balances of pension fund + balance of DRF)	+ 2500.00*
	Overall budgetary surplus (+) or Deficit (-) of the Government of India after taking into account contribution by Railways: (Dividend + balance of pension fund + balance of DRF)	- 10960.00 (-58551.00)**
	Budgetary Deficit (-) or surplus (+) of Govt. of India with a zero surplus in Railway Budget	- 12256.00 (-59847)***
D.	**Effect of Railway Budget with S.R.M.C./ L.R.M.C. Pricing on the Deficit (-) or Surplus (+) of the Government of India.**	
	1. Consequential Deficit (-) or surplus (+) of Government of India with L.R.M.C. Pricing adopted by Railways	- 12578.00
	2. Consequential deficit (-) or surplus (+) of Government of India with S.R.M.C. pricing adopted by Railways	14335.00
E.	**Consequential Levels of Surplus, Development Outlay, Net Revenues of Railways**	
	1. Needed surplus (+) in the railway budget with a return of 16% on total investment of Rs. 32212 crores in Railways	+ 512.00
	2. Plan of Railways that can be sustained by Railway Budget of the order of (1) above with a budgetary support of say Rs. 1000 crores with the 1993-94 level of dividend, DRF and pension fund.	+ 10791.00

3.	Needed Gross Revenue of Railways to sustain investment plan of (2) above.	+	25826.00
4.	Additional net revenues to be generated by restructured fares and freight charge to fulfill (3) over and above the 1992-93 (R) level of gross revenue of railways	+	7879.00
5.	Net Traffic Receipts (Surplus) on the basis of average cost pricing	+	3102.00
6.	Gross profit of Railways as per cent of total investment		9.6

* Estimated.

** Fiscal deficit.

*** Fiscal deficit.

If the Indian railways adopt marginal cost pricing, they will incur a heavy deficit. Under SRMC Pricing, the deficit will be Rs. 3375 crores. Under LRMC Pricing the deficit will be reduced to Rs. 1618 crores. With average cost pricing, there will be a marginal surplus of Rs. 1515 crores.

As said earlier, these deficits/surpluses have their effect on the overall budgetary position of the Government of India. The Railways, as per the present system, are making a contribution of Rs. 2500 crores to be General Budget (dividend balance of pension fund + balance of DRF), Not-withstanding this, the deficit of the Government of India even after taking into account the contribution by Railways will be Rs. 10960 crores. The fiscal deficit, however, touches Rs. 58551 crores. If the Railways have a zero surplus, the consequential deficit of the Government of India will rise to Rs. 12256 crores. Corresponding to this, the fiscal deficit will increase to Rs. 59847 crores. If the railways adopt SRMC pricing, the consequential deficit of the Government of India will be as high as Rs. 14335 crores. Even if they adopt LRMC pricing, the consequential deficit of the Government of India will rise to Rs. 12578 crores.

If the Railways work on 16% return on their total investment, they need a surplus of Rs. 5120 crores. With the budgetary support of Rs. 1269 crores ad 1996-97 level of dividend, the DRF and pension fund the outlay of the Railway Plan for 1996-97 is only Rs. 8130 crores. In order to sústain an outlay of Rs. 10791 crores gross revenue of the railways will have to be about Rs. 25826 crores. This would imply an additional gross revenue of Rs. 7879 crores may have to be generated by restructuring freight and fare charges over the above the 1995-96 (revised) level.

It goes without saying that neither the Indian Railways nor the Government of India can afford to incur deficits of the order mentioned above, especially at a time when the total investment in the country, both public and private sectors, will have to be very high for achieving a growth rate of exceeding 6% or the GDP.

This illustration seems to convince that any talk of SRMC pricing or LRMC pricing can only be of theoretical or academic value and such adventures can only push Indian Railways into the vicious circle of stagnant investment and rising deficits.

If SRMC pricing is adopted the urban sector and classes of people who are relatively better off get subsidised while in equity it ought to be the other way. If the surplus of the urban sector is utilised by financing the deficit caused by zero marginal cost pricing of the rural or uneconomic railways then it might improve the distribution of income. But, it cannot be easily known that users of railways in rural areas and uneconomic lines are the very people who deserve to be subsidised.

If full cost pricing is chosen with the emphasis on both marginal and total cost, then the totality of railway users does not benefit but the groups to which marginal cost applies receives a subsidy while the other which is subjected to more than average cost loses more. The advantage inherent in a system of building surpluses from the view point of distribution disappears.

Those who favour SRMC pricing feel that if the resulting

distribution is not acceptable to society, any attempt to redistribute those benefits by prices of railway services being greater or lesser that SRMC results in a smaller bundle of net profits. This need not necessarily happen. Spending the earning on projects which benefit all people or those whose needs are the greatest produces an off setting bundle of benefits. While discussing the merits of the SRMC pricing we should not forget that it connected with the efficient pricing of any form in achieving the redistributive aim. It is argued that pricing cannot achieve the distribution objective as the connection between railway user's charges levied to achieve income redistribution and those meant for achieving efficient use of railways is very remote and there is often no connection between the use of railways and the benefits received. This is not a strong point. After all, the border line between the use of public enterprise pricing and the use of taxes as a means of income distribution is a very thin one.[10] As the Indian case shows surplus in the railway budget can be increased by varying different kinds of user charges—on different qualities of services and activities. The only tax on passenger fare which was in existence some years ago has now been abolished. The super-fast charges or sleeper charges are being integrated with the main charges. These users' charges to not vary with the variation in the railway use, although, the main charge may decline under a tapering system over a long distances. Therefore, to say that they are independent of railway use is to say that a train or a track of the locomotive do not depreciate with use. It must be remembered when the railway assets are over-used with a feeling that no extra costs are incurred for doing so, we fall into the grap of greater wear out of the railway assets which calls for quicker replacement, thus attracting fresh investment liability/user charge liability very much earlier.

If pricing of railways is to be determined primarily by income distribution considerations, it is suggested that some growth can be sacrificed in order to achieve what society thinks a better distribution of income. The argument presupposes that subsidies bring about intended distribution. History, however, has provided instances of growth being promoted by transport facilities as negative.[11] For example in Ethiopia major transport improvements have led to substantial reduction in journey time and freight cost and substantial increase traffic, but not leading to any rapid growth. Brazil has been notoriously lack in transport charging but it has nevertheless achieved a faster rate of growth. In India itself there are instances where gauge conversion from meter to broad gauge and extension of the railway lines have not led to faster rate of growth of that region. On the contrary, losses are incurred. Therefore, we cannot assert undisputedly about any exact relationship between economic growth and transport pricing.

Subsidies, though intended to achieve a better distribution of income may produce consequences unfavourable for its realisation. This can happen in many ways. Firstly, when subsidies for railway users are a net addition to the budget-benefit, they bring about a further rise in prices. This recoils more on the lower income groups and subsidy gets neutralised by rising prices depriving the poorer sections the benefit of the subsidy. If the price rise exceeds the amount of the subsidy. If the price rise exceeds the amount of the subsidy. If the price rise exceeds the amount of the subsidy, they are made worse off, while the richer class, the profiteers, are favoured. Secondly, cheaper railway user charges attract business from roads in rural and urban areas. In this case, the poor and middle class who are owner operators of single bus fleet may suffer. Thirdly, pleasure travel in India is within the reach of only richer class in society unlike the developed countries where they are within the means of the common man. Therefore, substitution of travel intensive travel consumption goods for other goods or services induced by the subsidies will confirm more blessings only on the richer classes. There are some of subsidised pricing which stimulate growth and help raising the income of lower strata. For instance, mobility of factors and finished goods caused by cheaper railway transport facilities the development of rural areas. This creates work opportunities of landless labourers and others who are unemployed or under-employed.

The divergence between marginal cost and the price caused by market imperfections and externalities make price determination primarily by consideration of economic efficiency unsatisfactory. So also pricing railways with a primary regard for redistributive function produces inefficiencies due to basic attribute of the transport service and concealed incidence of railway user charges. Graff aruged that a public enterprise can be expected to set a price with regard for its effect on allocation of resources as well as on the distribution of wealth.[12]

At this point discussions can be endless about how this should be achieved and what is the ideal combination. The alternatives are; maximise the objective function of efficiency with redistributionable constraints or maximise the objective function of redistribution with efficiency in resource allocation constraints or some intermediate combination. All that can be said is the just as some efficiency can be scarified for the sake of better distribution of income, some inequity may also be tolerated if it is functional to efficiency. It is greater output and employment which the faster growth of the Indian Economy brings about that will rise the incomes at the lower end of the ladder. This is a more effective means than subsidies on railway transport prices to reduce income inequalities. Therefore, while both allocative efficiency and redistribution of income must influence policy, the redistributive objective must be considered secondary, in the matter of railway transport pricing.

From the above it will be clear that neither marginal cost pricing nor full cost pricing of railway services can achieve all the objectives of economic policy. Nevertheless pricing of some form is a better regulator because of its additional advantage of objectivity. If the issue is to guide the consumers to make an efficient use of railways, an ideal solution is given by marginal cost pricing. But it conflicts with issues of subsidised *versus* non-subsidised operation. Moreover, this calls for detailed information and cost which are lacking in railways and suitable charging mechanisms are yet to get developed. Therefore, given the need to avoid deficits and to generate larger surplus for investment in modernisation and expansion of railway network, the case for giving greater weightage for redistributive function alongwith allocative efficiency appears not desirable. Some form of full cost pricing (keeping also in view marginal costs in some line) with a rate of return adequate for investment in such a way as to prevent the railway network from becoming a bottleneck to a faster growth of the Indian Economy is to be advocated. The level of railway user charges that is commensurate with such pricing can give an idea of the optimal level of railway pricing.

Obviously this marks a departure from the ideal of marginal cost pricing. The emphasis will be, when given the institutional framework, losses arising from inefficient allocation, must as far as possible be minimised for competing modes of transport—the railways and the roads. The resulting losses in allocative efficiency under full cost plus pricing are to be weighed against the benefits from increased railway facilities causing lesser dislocation for the growth of the Indian Economy and the consequences of larger budgetary deficits arising from greater losses in the Railway Budget.

COSTS AND PRODUCTIVITY

In the pricing of Railway services, whether under marginal cost pricing or full cost pricing, the cost of service turns out to be very crucial. The Indian Railways have not evolved any norms for determining the cost. Under ordinary working expenses, all expenditure incurred by them for operating Railways are taken as valid expenditure. The system does not take into cognisance the optimal productivity in relation to the capital invested and the capacity of the work force employed. Consequently, whatever expenditures are incurred, they are all treated as 'inevitable working expenses'. This approach has been criticised as not rational by the Committee on Railway Fare and Freight,[13] which submitted its Report to the Ministry of Railways in December, 1993. Certain recommendations have been made for developing norms on expenditure and also for minimising wasteful and infractuous expenditure.

If this is done, there is scope for lowering the prices of the Railway services without sacrificing the quantum and quality. I do not go into the details of this approach here. I will only content myself by giving some broad indicators of productivity for selected years. These are given in Table 1.

TABLE 1
Utilisation of Railway Assets
Indicators of Productivity for Selected Years

Indicators	*1985-86*	*1990-91*	*1991-92*
1	2	3	4
Basic Indicators			
1. Gross tonne Kms. Moved per Kg. of tractive effort (GTKMs)	3.114	3.873	4.026
2. Net tonne Kms per engine hour (NTKMs)	8.812	10.393	10.911
3. Net tonne Kms per route Km (NTKMs in lakhs)	54.6	63.0	66.3
4. Passenger Kms per route Km (PKMs in lakhs)	58.8	71.2	75.8
5. Wagon Kms per wagon day	97.8	110.5	113.2
6. Net Tonne Kms per Wagon day (NTKMs)	1.296	1.407	1.439
7. Investment (cumulative) (Rs. crores)			
(a) at current prices	11.492	22.000	24.808
(b) at constant (1985-86) prices*	11.492	14.399	14.386
Productivity per Rs. 100 crores investment**			
8. Gross tonne Kms per kg of tractice effort per Rs. 100 crores investment (GTKMs)	27.10	26.90	27.99
9. Net tonne Kms. per engine hour per Rs. 100 crores of investment (NTKMs)	76.68	72.18	75.84
10. Net tonne Kms. per route Km per Rs. 100 crores of investment (NTKMs)	47.511	43.753	46.086
11. Passenger Kms. per route Km per Rs. 100 crores of investment (PKMs)	51.166	49.448	52.690
12. Wagon Kms. per wagon day per Rs. 100 crores of investment (WKMs)	0.85	0.77	0.79
13. Net tonne Kms. per wagon day per Rs. 100 crores of investment (NTKMs)	11.28	9.77	10.02

* WIIR Index with base as 1985-86.
** 1985-86 prices.

Sources: Indian Railways:
(i) Annual Report and Accounts 1991-92.
(ii) Year Book 1991-92.
(iii) Facts and Figures 1991-92.

In the aggregate, an intensive utilisation of the Railway assets shows an improvement in productivity in indicators like Gross Ton Kms. moved per Kg. of tractive effort; net Kms. per engine hour; wagon kms. per wagon day. However, when related to investment of say a block Rs. 100 crores, the improvement in productivity in respect of the above mentioned indicators shows either a marginal decline or negligible increase or near stagnancy during the period 1986-92.

In recent years, budgetary support to Railways has been dwindling without giving the Railways complete autonomy in its functioning. Maintaining the same old type of ministerial control, Indian Railways are asked to mobilise more of resources internally so that they can have a larger plan budget for their development. It would appear that unless the Indian Railways are made to function like commercial enterprises, rationalising their responsibility for various items of expenditure like welfare expenditure, police force expenditure, and the social costs to be borne by the Railways for cross subsidisation, the Railway finance will continue to be distorted and fail to produce the necessary internal resources including intentional surpluses to support a development plan that would show the Railways in a much better light. The resources crunch has held back the pace of development of Railways as a cheaper means of transport, apart from being more eco-friendly. On the other hand, if they are to mobilise more internal resources this can be done by raising the fare and freight charges irrespective of whether they are rational and are not likely to affect the traffic. Already, the Railways have lost more than 50 per cent of the freight traffic to the roads. Even bulk items like coal, iron and steel, sugar, cement, fertilisers are now moving by roads which consume more of the foreign exchange due to oil imports apart from contributing to the heavy congestion on roads and to environmental pollution. In fact, this had given rise to sub-optimal transport modemix and if allowed to continue in this manner in the coming years, it cannot but have disastrous consequences to the country. The quality of the Railway services is getting poorer. In making this observation one has to take note of the overall work and the feeling of the freight customers and passengers. A few trains like Shatabdi and Rajdhani do not cater to the masses of the population. No goods-train run on schedule and trans-shipment losses and pilferage are on the rise. The pet answer is that goods are carried at the risk of the owners. This is, indeed, a very depressing performance.

SOCIAL COSTS/BURDEN IN RAILWAY FINANCE

I am not going into the fare and freight structure or to the areas where infractuous and wasteful expenditures are presently found. I have only touched upon the absolute need to make the Railways function as a commercial enterprise giving them autonomy for pricing and investment policies. In this context, I would argue that the present policy of making a commercial enterprise like the Indian Railways to earn more revenues from the freight segment to make up the losses on the passenger traffic segment is not conductive for optimal efficiency of the Railways.

Railways lose from uneconomic branch lines, carrying low rated commodities at confessional rates, carrying export items at below costs, providing coaching services in sub-urban and non-sub-urban passenger traffic at below cost and in the sub-urban passenger services in metropolitan cities like Bombay, Calcutta and Chennai where they operate Electric Multiple Unit and Non-Electric Multiple Unit Services.

Table 2 presents the estimated losses incurred by the Indian Railways by way of social costs by reasons and other expenditure reported under social costs.

It will be seen that the burden of the social costs (subsidy) has risen from Rs. 1980 cores in 1989-90 to Rs. 2215 crores in 1992-93. There is a small reduction in the next year to Rs. 2082 crores. Railways were showing their expenditure on welfare (expenditure on medical, housing, educational facilities, etc.) and the expenditure on police force under social costs. Consequently, according to them the social burden was Rs. 2480 crores in 1989-90 reaching Rs. 2865 in 1993-94. The Committee on Railway Fare and Freight Committee headed by me did not agree for including welfare costs and expenditure on police

TABLE 2

(Rupees in Crores)

Sl. No.	Reasons	1980-90	1990-91	1991-92	1992-93	1993-94
1	2	3	4	5	6	7
A.	**Estimated Losses incurred by the IR/Social Costs by Reasons and other Expenses reported under Social Cost**					
1.	Losses from uneconomic branch lines	107.00	107.00	104.00	121.00	146.00
2.	Losses on low rates commodities* carried at concessional rates (below cost)	152.61	236.33	321.7	215.02	65.42
3.	Carrying iron-ore meant for exports at below cost	30.01 (36.69)[a]	12.36	62.99 (71.05)[b]	Nil(c)	Nil
4.	Losses on coaching service (Sub-urban and non-sub-urban passenger traffic, parcel, luggage etc.) due to below cost pricing (including concessions to students and other categories and users) of which	1683.22	1836.64	1730.29	1914.15	1665.60
4a.	Sub-urban passenger services in Bombay, Calcutta and Chennai operating EMU and non-EMU Services**	197.62	207.31	212.69	NA	205.44
5.	Total losses arising from below cost fare and freight charge (1+2+3+4)	1979.52	2222.33	2227.13	2250.17	2082.46
B.	**Other Expenses**					
6.	Expenditure on medical, housing, educational facilities, etc.	308.71	340.05	364.25	403.95[d]	473.27

7. Expenditure on police force	191.98	201.25	220.33	249.88	309.96
8. Expenditure that reduces railway surpluses (6+7)	500.69	541.30	584.58	653.83	783.23

* Foodgrains, salt, fodder, sugarcane, fruits, vegetables, edible oils and other commodities.

** The breakup of this loss is not available in the Explanatory Memorandum on the Railway Budget. However, in the Indian Railways Year Book such a breakup is available and is adopted here. It appears that the figures in the Year Book are more or less based on actual receipts and computed costs.

Notes: Losses incurred due to concessions given for Postal Department and Defence Department for 1991-92 are estimated by RFFC at Rs. 2.0 crores and Rs. 40.50 crores respectively. They are included under Sl. No. 2 and 4.

(a) Included loss of Rs. 6.65 crores due to carrying other ores at a concessional rate.

(b) Included loss of Rs. 8.06 crores due to carrying other ones at a concessional rate.

(c) Consequent to the withdrawal of concessions, not less is incurred from this item.

(d) Railway Budget: NA=Not Available.

Source: Explanatory Memorandum on the Railway Budget 1990-91, 1991-92, 1992-93, 1993-94 and 1994-95. Indian Railways Year Book, Directorate of Statistics and Economics, Railway Board.

protection force as social burden. Since the submission of the Committee's Report in December, 1993, the Indian Railways have been showing the expenditure on welfare and police force separately, but yet in the Chapter on 'Social Cost'. It is necessary to rationalise the subsidy on the Railway services once we want them to function as commercial enterprise with an obligation to earn a profit of say 16 per cent in order to sustain themselves. Therefore, the Committee headed by me has recommended that where the Government justifiably wants the user charges to be below cost, the responsibility for such a benefit should be borne by the 'general budget'. The enterprise should not be asked to absorb the losses out of its own earnings. It is, however, to be noted that in the case of the commuter traffic and the sub-urban Railway services, it is not possible to adopt full cost plus pricing. The commuters are entitled to good and reasonably cheaper transport facilities. This may have to be subsidised by the Government through the budget. Even where subsidies are justified, it would appear desirable that some ceiling is imposed in the matter of the subsidy. It is generally felt that not more than 1/3 of the costs need be subsidised with some flexibility. If this is not done, the chances of Railway finances being stable and be in a position to earn adequate surpluses for their development are, indeed, bleak.

RESTRUCTURE RAILWAY FINANCE

It is interesting to know the practice which obtains in some of the countries like Great Britain, Germany, France, Switzerland where Railways perform a major role in the transport network. In these foreign countries, while the Railways have their own pricing policy based on cost plus pricing, the Governments of these countries give subsidy from the 'General Budget' to the Railways where their services are priced at below cost. Table 3 sows details of the total passenger earnings, subsidy given to the Railways and the percentage of subsidy to the total revenue earnings.

TABLE 3

Percentage of Subsidy to Total Revenue is given by the Government for Selected Foreign Railways, 1992-93

Sl. No.	*Railway System*	*Passenger earnings*	*Subsidy*	*Total Revenue earnings*	*Percentage of subsidy to total revenue*
1	2	3	4	5	6
1.	British Railways*	2010.0	809.0	2602.0	31.09
2.	Swiss Federal Rlys. SWFr	1693.0	2439.0	6279.0	38.8
3.	German Federal Rlys. DM (DB)	7574.0	22683.0	33416.0	67.9
4.	French National Rlys. FFr. Rlys. (SNCF)	31356.0	42900.0	89247.0	48.1

* Excluding inter-city services.

Note: Figs. in columns 3 to 5 are in millions of currency units of the respective countries i.e., Stg. Pound £ SW Fr., DM and French Dr. (FFr).

Source: James World Railways, 1994-95.

I will be seen that Railways in Great Britain, Germany, France and Switzerland receive subsidy from the Government ranging from 31% of 68% of their total revenue earnings. Germany tops the list with a 68% subsidy given to the German Federal Railways. French National Railways come next with 48% subsidy receiving from the Government. Swiss Federal Railways receive 39% subsidy and the British Railways got 31% subsidy before their privatisation.

Therefore, Indian Railway finances should get restructured to suit the requirements of the commercial enterprise. Taking the total financial scenario of our country further continuance of indiscrete subsidies and neglecting efficiency in financial management of the Railways can only lead to further destablishing and destroying the Government's one of the most successful pubic enterprises like the Indian Railways. The resource requirements of the Indian Railways are enormous and the restructuring of their finances brooks no further delay.

Notes and References

1. *Supra*, p. 45.
2. See Stwart Joy, 'Railway Costs and Planning' in Journal of Transport Economics and Policy, Vol. XIII, No. 1, January 1989.
3. Cf: H.M.S.O. Report on Transport Cost, 1968.
4. See R. Turvey, "Marginal Cost", *The Economic Journal*, Vol. LXXIV, No. 134, June 1969, pp. 282-98.
5. See Marcel Boitem, "Peak-Load Pricing" in James R. Nelson (Ed.) Marginal Cost Pricing in Practice, 1964.
6. See Stwart Joy, *Op. cit.*
7. See D.M. Nanjundappa, Road User Taxation and Road Finance, Popular Prakashan, Bombay, 1973.
8. See Ewen Michael and Mauren Rimmer, 'Eliminating Railway Deficits the Effects for Australia, in Journal of Transport and Economic Policy, January 1991.
9. *Supra*, p. 32.
10. Cf: A.R. Prest, Transport Economics in Developing Countries, p. 36.
11. See Gerard "Transport" in H.J. Habkkuk and M.M. Preson (Eds.) Cambridge Economic History of Europe", Vol. VI part I, 1965 pp. 212-70; Robert W. Fogel "Railway Roads as an Analogy to the space effort: Some Economic Aspects" in *Economic Journal*, Vol. LXXVI, March 1966, pp. 16-48.
12. See J. De. V. Graff, Theoretical Welfare Economics, 1957, p. 155.
13. Chaired be me.

CHAPTER 5

Financial Sector Reforms in India and China: A Comparative Study

ALAK GHOSH

INTRODUCTION

The fastest growing sector of the Indian economy during the eighties was the Services Sector particularly Public Administration and Defence. The GDP growth rate during the eighties was almost 5.5 per cent per anuum. From 1981-82 to 1985-86, the growth rate was 5.06 per cent. During the next five years (1985-86 to 1989-90) the average per annum growth rate reached the high figure of 5.31 per cent. For the period between 1985-86 to 1991-92 the average per annum growth rate was 5.13 per cent. The main strategy for achieving this high growth rate of the eighties depended on increasing Government expenditure, undertaking deficit financing and expanding the outlays on Public Administration and Defence.

The liberalisation programme under economic reforms, started by the Rao Government in July 1991, continued the acceleration of GDP growth so that by 1995-96 the growth rate was 7 per cent.

According to the World Bank's latest (1996) country study (India) the growth performance of India's service sector in 1996-97 is 8.1 per cent whereas for agriculture the rate is 2.3 per cent and for industry it is almost the same as the services. This is expected since the reforms of the investment system, exchange rate, trade regimes and of the tax structure give a spurt to the growth process and brings about widespread ramifications. In 1985-86, the service sectors contribution to GDP was about 30 per cent and in 1995-96 this contribution has gone upto 40 per cent as announced by India's Finance Minister while presenting the 1997-98 Union Budget. The flow of foreign capital in an accelerated manner, brings in both foreign direct investment and portfolio investment. This requires the expansion, structural adjustment and revamping of the financial sector. In short, the growth of the real sector, during the process of economic reforms, cannot be sustained unless it is accompanied by adequate financial sector reforms. The purpose of this paper is to make a comparative analysis of economic reforms in India and China with special reference to changes that have occurred in the financial sector particularly banking and insurance.

COMPARATIVE ANALYSIS OF ECONOMIC REFORMS IN INDIA AND CHINA—LESSONS FOR INDIA

Economic reforms in China were gradual and where spread over a long period starting after Deng Xiao Ping's political ascendancy in 1978. The reforms in China come under three phases (Sachs and Woo, 1994). The first phase of the reforms began with China's economic take-off in 1978-79 and extended upto 1981-82. China's economic take-off during this phase heavily depended on rural liberalisations. For the first time, a portion of the farm output began to be sold at market-determined prices in free agricultural markets. Simultaneously, Township and Village Governments were increasingly encouraged to establish Township and Village Enterprises (TVEs) for the production and sale of Industrial Commodities outside the Central Plan. TVEs gradually gained in strength and in 1995-96 the TVEs produced a little over 61% of the Industrial output in China.

The second phase of reforms started in early eighties and aimed at globalisation and internationalisation. Though the Chinese economy began to open up for international trade and capital, the initial market opening began around 1979 with the devaluation of highly over-valued exchange rate. In fact, devaluation of exchange rate was a greater magnitude in China than in India during the period of economic reforms. Trade liberalisation progressed gradually throughout the 1980s; exporting firms were permitted to hold a large portion of foreign exchange earned by them. Further devaluation of exchange rate took place in the coastal regions of Ziangsu, Zheziang and Guandong associated with the establishment of Special Economic Zones (SEZs) linking them to Hong Kong and Taiwan. Finally, by 1990 rudimentary foreign exchange markets were established in China particularly in the Coastal regions. All these steps paved the way for foreign direct investment.

The third phase of the economic reforms concentrated on the development of Urban industry and started around 1984-85. This set of reforms aimed at giving greater autonomy for industrial units, including greater freedom to determine contract prices and select inputs and outputs. Both the workers and the managers obtained extra incentives by having their salaries linked to the index of "Enterprise Performance" which is very similar to what is known as "Productivity-linked Wage" in a capitalist set-up like India. State enterprises were modeled into a two-track system conceptually similar to that a household farmers. The state sector enterprises had to deliver a portion of their output to the Government, while the remaining portion would be sold freely in the open market.

It is to be noted here that three phases of economic reforms in China extended over more than a decade are still proceeding and producing results. The Chinese experiment with economic reforms during the last 18 years show the merit of "Gradualism" over "Stock therapy" treatment. In fact, China has proved the superiority of "Gradualism and Experimentation" to rapid "Top-Down Reforms" based on a strategy of "Big-Bang" policy.

The lesson, which India can learn from the Chinese experience of economic reforms is that in a big country with huge land area and explosive population plus regional differences. "Experimentation and Gradualism" are perhaps better than the "Big-Bang" policy of rapid liberalisation and quick privatisation. Therefore, those who criticise the economic reforms as slow and not producing quick results after the initial outbursts of success, should ponder for a while and make a serious study of the Chinese experiment of economic reforms which enabled China to achieve an average growth rate of 13.3% between 1991-92 and 1995-96.

The Chinese experiment also clearly demonstrates the wisdom of starting the reform process in agriculture before the industrial reforms. It was noticed that by 1981 there was a massive, almost spontaneous, giving up of collective property in agriculture. It is interesting to find that in 1983 the "Peoples Communes" were formally liquidated. The individual household farms reigned supreme form 1984 onwards and served as the main basis of agricultural production. This, in twin, paved the way for the emergence of the TVEs which ultimately became the backbone of industrial production in China. In contrast to that, Indian economic reforms, even after six years, has not accomplished comprehensive reform programme for agriculture on which 70 per cent of the Indian population depend for their livelihood.

The Chinese experiment of reforms, based on "Gradualism" and "Selective Approach" indicates that most of China's rapid growth came from two major areas. Firstly, in rural regions where the non-state enterprises known as TVEs, increasingly prospered and contributed little over 61 percent of the industrial output by 1995-96. Secondly the coastal areas, where market openings established a link with Hong Kong and Taiwan experienced an export boom and also a huge inflow of foreign direct investment. Incidentally, it should be mentioned here that the areas heavily loaded with State enterprises fared badly specially from the mid eighties and became less important for contributing to industrial production and economic growth. Thus it is evident that the direction of reforms is more important than the speed of reforms.

It is, however, heartening to note that since 1991, the State Owned Enterprises (SOEs) have become subject to market forces and the managers have started to respond to these forces. This is a case in point which should be specially noted when we think of revamping the Public Sector Units (PSUs) in India. As in China, so also in India. The SOEs and PSUs cannot disappear overnight. They will have to remain and mould themselves into more efficient units so that they can effectively compete with private enterprises in a market friendly economy.

Chinese TVEs are highly modernised small scale units and can be compared with sophisticated and mechanised units in Taiwan and Hong Kong. In contrast, India small-scale industries, which have grown under the protective umbrella, have not been technologically upgraded, and have gradually lost ground to medium-sized industries which depend on superior technology and utilize better R & D facilities. It is high time that we make a serious study of Chinese experiment revolving round the successful growth of TVEs and formulate a comprehensive programme for revamping India's small-scale industries. It should be remembered that small-scale industries have a better employment potential than the medium and large scale enterprises and, therefore proper development of the small-scale sector is vital for India where poverty and unemployment are the two main obstacles to development.

Evolution of Institutions, Markets, and Instruments of the Financial Sector in China and India

Like reforms in the real sector of the Chinese economy financial (mainly banking reforms did not proceed along a well-planned, comprehensive blueprint but instead, has been marked by gradualism and pragmatism. It is useful to remember here that reforms in China has been evolutionary rather than revolutionary. The size and diversity of the Chinese economy, as well as, Deng Xiao Ping's insistence on decentralisation of decision making in the early stages of the reform process have promoted the Chinese policy makers to adopt small-scale experimental approaches which subsequently were extended to cover the national scene. Thus, reforms both in the real sector and the financial sector of the Chinese economy have been characterised by gradualism, selectivism and pragmatism.

The most spectacular change took place in 1992 when the Communist Party officially recognised that the market system was not incompatible with the ideals of socialism and subsequently proclaimed the idea of establishing a 'socialist market economy'. Incidentally, it may be mentioned here that the term "market socialism" was first used by Professor Oscar Lange in the fifties but the Polish Government never took the concept seriously while working with the ideals of a socialist economy. The concept of a " Socialist Market Economy" points to an economy where market mechanisms govern economic interactions but the public sector maintains ownership of the most important means of production. Chinese have used the "market socialism strategy" as the main tool of liberalisation. The Chinese economic reforms strategy during the early nineties highlighted financial reforms as the main element in attempts to evolve efficient financial markets in order to strengthen the Government's capacity to bring about structural adjustment and macroeconomic management, utilising mainly indirect monetary instruments.

Development of Financial Institutions

In the sphere of banking reforms, institution building began in the early 1980s with the establishment of a two-tier banking system. Initially, the apex bank of China, which is known as the Peoples Bank of China (PBC), was vested with the dual responsibility of central banking and commercial banking. Gradually, the PBC gave up its commercial banking activity. In 1984 the PBC became China's central bank but the evolution of central banking in the true sense of the term was slow, gradual and done in an experimental manner.

It is some what strange to find that, in spite of the existence of a Central Bank of China, the Credit Plan continued to be the kingpin on which rested the operation of monetary and credit policies. The Credit Plan was implemented through a set of credit quotas for each bank and direct bank financing of enterprises. The Credit Plan dominated the financial scenario since it met local and sectoral financial needs done from the bottom up (i.e., from the base to the top). This seriously hampered the autonomy of the Chinese Central Bank and the ability of the PBC to efficiently manage monetary developments. This type of experimentalism and lack of clear cut monetary policy outfit continued till 1992-93 when the work on a new Central bank Law as taken up seriously, and the Chinese Central Banking Law as formally enacted. This gave the PBC the legal foundation to operate in market friendly environment under the leadership of State Council.

The absence of a solid legislative underplanning seriously impaired Chinese financial sector reforms between 1984 and 1995. From the mid eighties, when emerging market forces started to have an impact and financial system expanded in a somewhat unsystematic manner, the PBC's relationship with the state owned commercial banks was neither intimate nor effective. It is disheartening to note that the PBC had to struggle a lot to establish its authority over the commercial banks and the newly emerging sections of the financial systems. In fact, the tendency to decnetralised decision making and China's political administrative structure, together with the absence of a legislative back-up, initially gave the local and regional authorities more influence over PBC branches and branches of the state-owned specialised commercial banks than those exercised by PBCs own headquarters. It was as late as 1995 that this unsatisfactory and hotch-potch situation was remedied by the enactment of the 1995 Central Bank Law. The 1995 Central Banking Act firmly established the authority of the PBC's head office over all its branches and, as a result financial sector reforms could progress further along an easy and systematic path.

Turning to India, we find that the development of the institution of Central Banking was done in a systematic manner and with easy confidence. The Indian Central Bank, known as the Reserve Bank of India (RBI), was established in 1935 under the Reserve Bank Act, 1934. The RBI, after its establishment, took over the function of currency issue from the Government and that of credit control and monetary management from the Imperial Bank of India which was performing the dual function of commercial banking and central banking before RBI came into existence. The RBI, which originally started as a shareholder's bank, became a state-owned and State-controlled Central Bank form 1st January 1949.

Indian commercial banks (both in the private and public sectors) are controlled and regulated by the RBI under the power vested to it by the Banking Regulations Act, 1949. It is interesting to note that from November 1951 (i.e. almost forty years before the reforms started in India), the RBI sat on the saddle with credit reins in its hand and gradually assumed a firm grip over money and credit. In fact, the RBI saw to it that the market was getting as much money as the central bank chose not as much as market wanted. Unlike China, the Indian Central Bank, developed on the model of the Bank of England, had a firm footing as an institution and was functioning more or less effectively even during the pre-reform years. The only point common with China is that the RBI was gradually loosing autonomy and was getting more and more tied up to the apron-strings of the Banking Department of the Finance Ministry of the Government of India.

The economic reforms, which started in India in July 1991. has sought to do away with controls, regulations, licensing and bureaucratic red-tapism. In this new era of liberalisation, where market forces play a dominant role, it is essential that Indian central bank have a substantial autonomy in decision-making and gets itself free from the control of the Finance Ministry of the Government of India. In this connection it is worthwhile mentioning that the committee for Financial Sector Reform, (headed by Mr. M. Narasimham) which submitted their Report to the Government within five months of the starting of the Reform process, have made important recommendations for the thorough revamping and restructuring of the Indian banking system, particularly commercial banking. The Narasimham Committee has emphasized that both Central Banking and commercial banking should strive for operational flexibility and autonomy in decision making. In China this will be difficult since China has achieved economic liberalisation without political liberalisation. But why should it be difficult in India when the Indian Government professes that they are trying to achieve simultaneously economic and political liberalisation? In short the institution of central banking has developed in a pragmatic and gradual manner both in India and China but the development of central banking was almost complete in India before the reform process started whereas in China the development process was done in an experimental and unsystematic manner during the eighties and early nineties. It was only in 1995 with the enactment of the Central Banking Act, the PBC obtained a solid foundation and could embark on the path of monetary management and development in a smooth and systematic manner.

As we have already seen monetary policy in China remains guided by the credit plan during the early years of the reform process. But the effectiveness of the Credit Plan was diminishing since the late eighties mainly due to the fact that its institutional coverage has lagged behind the expansion of the banking sector.

In the early reform years China opted for specialised public sector banks. First, there is Bank of China (BOC) which is the biggest commercial banks undertaking both direct and indirect leading functions. BOC is a State owned bank and can be compared with India's biggest public sector bank—the State Bank of India. The other three State-owned specialised banks in China are really development banks from the conceptual point of view. In the field of agricultural finance we have in China the Agricultural Bank of China (ABC) of course, ABC can be compared with the apex agricultural bank in India known as National Bank for Agriculture and Rural Development (NABARD). Unlike NABARD, the ABC has a wide network of branches and concentrate on direct lending for agricultural purposes. However, like NABARD, ABC, does not under take refinancing.

Next we have in China another specialised commercial bank which is known as the Peoples' Construction Bank of China

(PCBC). This state-owned bank provides funds for both housing construction and, in a small way, for infrastructural development. In India we have the apex body known as the National Housing Bank (NHB) which is fully owned by the Reserve Bank of India and which provides refinance facilities to both private sector and public sector Housing Banks. In India, during the reform period there has been phenomenal growth of housing construction particularly in the bigger and medium-sized cities and there has been a spurt in the lending activities of both public sector and private sector Housing Banks. Like China, India does not have specialised bank for financing infrastructual sector. It is interesting to note here that, in accordance to the 1996-97 budget announcement, India has recently established Infrastructural Development Finance Company (IDFC). IDFC is a joint sector body. It acts as a direct lender, as a refinancing institution and as a provider of financial guarantees. China has no exclusive specialised body for financing the infrastructural sector, and therefore, it has to rely on PCBC for direct and indirect finding of infrastrucutural projects. Of course, during the ten year period (1984-94), the Chinese Government permitted selected new banks to operate alongside the State-owned banks particularly in the coastal regions of Ziangsu, Zheziang and Guandong. The selected banks functioned as local area Banks and have indirect links with the foreign banks. They meet the financial needs of the growing sectors of the economy.

Last of all, we have a specialised bank in China for providing Industrial fiance. The name of this banks is Industrial and Commercial Bank of China (ICBC). ICBC undertakes mixed banking function and provides direct and indirect finance for industrial development. But it should be remembered that the ICBC is not like Industrial Development Bank of India (IDBI), and does not provide refinancing facilities to the State-financial Institutions. As noted earlier, new Local Area Banks are growing in number not only in coastal regions but also in areas with high growth potential and dominated by Township and Village Enterprises (TVEs) which have done extremely well and at present distributes 60 percent of China industrial production. It is interesting to note that the profits of the TVEs are channelised by these Local Area Banks for local infrastructural development.

In 1995, the New Commercial Banking Law was enacted in China and this gave a formal footing to the growth of the Local Area Banks. During the second half of the 1980s, a growing network of Non-Bank Financial Institution (NBFIs) emerged in China. The enactment of China's new Commercial Banking Law in 1995 somewhat reduced the importance of the Credit Plan and has given more freedom to both local area commercial banks and NBFIs in different fields of operations.

The emergence of the NBFI sector has surely enriched the financial scenario in China. It has also produced challenges to the Government. New legislation, designed to regulate and streamline NBFIs, was formulated in 1996. The Government having realised that uncontrolled NBFIs pose a threat to monetary policy, has now include certain types of NBFIs in its Credit Plan to ensure an adequate control system.

In India, side by side, with development of commercial banking, there has been a phenomenal growth of NBFIs, particularly hire purchase companies, chit funds, investment companies and mutual savings banks. In the last thirty years Reserve Bank of India is disparately trying to control the growth of undesirable types of NBFIs. The Reserve Bank's recent directives put mainly a series of curbs on the undesirable activities of hire-purchase and housing finance companies. It is true that NBFIs activate idle savings but at the same time, an unregulated growth of NBFIs seriously impairs effective monetary management.

Development of Financial Markets

Turning to the evolution, growth and structural changes in money and capital markets we find that China is a late starter. The foundation of Bombay Stock Exchange (BSE) in India was laid in 1917. Almost simultaneously stock exchanges were established in Calcutta and Ahmedabad. Today there is a chain of stock exchanges located in all important big towns and financial centres in India. In contrast to this, China's first stock market opened in Shanghai in September 1986 and a few months later another stock exchange started functioning in

Shenzhen. The local authorities in Shanghai and Shenzhen initially encouraged the growth of stock exchanges in their cities without support from the National Government. It was only in 1990 that the Chinese Government gave recognition to Shanghai's stock market as the nations major successful stock exchange experiment. Next year in 1991 the Government also recognised the development of the Shenzhen stock market. Between 1991 and 1996 stock exchange experiments were undertaken in six other important business towns in Ziangsu, Zheziang and Guandong—all located in the Special Economic Zones (SEZs). In the Chinese case the growth of the secondary section of the capital market has been more marked than the development of the primary market during the reform period. China, in the sphere of money and capital market development depended more on small-scale experiment approaches which later were adopted on national scale after support and approval came from the National Government. Instances of the selective approach in the financial sector include the starting of local inter-bank sectors in selected cities in 1986 and secondary markets in Government securities in six coastal towns in 1988. Other towns were permitted to undertake this course of action after the Government had received sufficient signals that the initial experiment has been successful.

Turning to India, we find that the growth in the capital market in India received a significant momentum during the 1980's. During the decade of eighties growing number of investors were attracted because of broadening of the base with increasing diversity of financial instruments floated in the market. In the first two years of economic reforms in India we witnessed a liberalised scenario characterised by freeing of interest rates and greater amount of characterised by freeing of interest rates and greater amount of marketisation. Indian stock markets were booming at an extraordinary speed and appeared to be backing Manmohan Singh's economic reforms to the hilt. But it was so discovered that the excessive boom in share prices were mainly speculative in character and there was unusual siphoning of money form the securities market to the stock market. In fact, the Sluice-gates between the money markets and the stock markets opened up and, ultimately the unusual boom in the stock market came to a jerky halt within a year of the start of the economic reforms in India.

Focussing the spotlight on the foreign exchange market, we find that this market is still in an embryonic form of China. It was only in 1986 that China introduced a "Swap" market in foreign exchange in business transaction. Though swap centers dealing with exchange retention rights so as to improve the use of foreign exchage in transactions started functioning since 1986, some of the regulations under the State Administration for exchange control continued, The National Foreign Exchange Market was created by the Chinese Government, particularly for the coastal region, as late as 1994. As a result, from 1995 the exchange rate between the different "Swap" centres ("Swap" rates) were successfully unified. This gave a solid foundation to the Chinese National Foreign Exchange Market. Ultimately, the official rate and the swap rate were unified from 1996.

In India the foreign exchange regulations were speedily relaxed during the Reform Period. The method of partial convertibility, based on the dual exchange rate system, was the first move towards the freely convertible Rupee. Rupee became fully convertible on trade account (though not on capital account) from the 1993-94 financial year. Thus, India current A/c convertibility in contract to China, has made long strides in the sphere of free foreign exchange market dominated by competitive forces. The Reserve Bank of India played the role of a good manager and facilitator in maintaining a parity between the free market rate and the official rate.

Evolution of Monetary and Financial Instruments

We shall now briefly discuss evolution of monetary and financial instruments. The development of money and financial market presupposes the free operation of the price-*cum*-interest rate mechanism. In contrast to India, freeing of interest rates was a far cry in China. The absence of nationally organised money market one of the weak features of China's financial sector even in the early 1990s—is related to its slow start on interest rate liberalisation together with a lack of modern payments and settlement infrastructure. The lack of nationally integrated inter-bank and money markets has seriously affected efforts to achieve the transition from direct to indirect instruments of monetary policy. The Chinese authorities have, therefore, regulate liquidity by adjusting reserve requirements and utilising the PBC's lending facilities for banks while maintaining relatively stable interest rates. From 1995 when the Central Bank Law was enacted, the Variable Ratio (VRR) became the main instrument of monetary Control in China. From 1996, the PBC, with a solid legal foundation, started to operate the VRR weapon in a market-environment under the leadership of the state council. Since 1992, with a large number of local inter-bank centres, there are more and more operations with commercial bills particularly in trade and commerce which takes place in Special Economic Zones. From 1991-92, branches of foreign banks were opened of SEZs. Credit quotas became more flexible and bank branches were permitting to have more freedom in determining their leading and deposit rates in SEZs than elsewhere in China. Consequently, economic growth in the SEZs has far outstripped that in the rest of the areas.

In India, during pre-reform period the financial system was characterised by an administered structure of interest rates. This system aimed at directing implicit subsidies to certain crucial sectors enabling them to get funds at concessional rates of interest. In India, with the starting of economic reforms for liberalisation and marketisation came the freeing of interest rates from July 1991. Very soon the interest rates on the convertible and non-convertible debentures became free. In a major move, the minimum lending rates system was abolished by the Reserve Bank of India (RBI) and the lending rates were freed in October 1994 for credit limits over Rs. 0.2 million. In India, on the recommendations of Narasimham Committee, the Cash Reserve Ratio (CRR) was systematically lowered during the Reform Period from 15 percent to 10 percent. The RBI in its latest credit policy (April 1997) has announced the removal of CRR on inter-bank liabilities. Banks have been allowed to evolve their own method for assessing working capital requirements for borrowers. The RBI-controlled maximum permissible bank finance has been scrapped. Banks will be allowed to extend loans to business firms against the shares held by them.

In the pre-reform period, Indian monetary policy was dominated by the Bank Rate instrument and Selective Credit Control (SSC), Open Market Operations (OMO), as an instrument of credit control, was relegated to the back ground and was transformed into an ancilliary tool of Governments debt management. Under the liberalised scenario, dominated by competitive market forces, OMO has staged a comeback. But both the Bank Rate weapon and the instrument of SCC are still important, For instance, in April 1997, the RBI lowered the Bank Rate by one percentage point from 12 per cent to 11 per cent. Subsequently in June 1997 the Bank Rate was reduced to 10 per cent for effective monetary management. In contrast to China, VRR gadget of credit control is gradually loosing its importance in the sphere of Indian monetary policy, specially after the announcement of the new credit policy in April 1997.

The development of new financial instruments in the Indian money market has broadened the market and has made it more active. The introduction of Participation Certificates (PCs) and both 182-Day and 364-Day Treasury Bills have immensely helped the development of Indian money market. Incidentally, it should be observed here that the growth and effective functioning of the Discount and Finance House of India (DFHI) which was established in April 1988, has strengthened the Indian money market. In short, there are more effective direct and indirect instruments for monetary control in India than in China. Freeing of interest rates have been more successful in India than China. This is mainly because India had an earlier start and followed an effective, and systematic monetary policy which was adopted to the needs of the liberalised scenario with great dexterity and skill. China's main disadvantage was that the monetary policy had to operate within the credit plan and a system of State regulation and control . Though China was a late starter, it struggled for financial sector development with experimental approaches some amount of success in certain spheres was achieved.

Four Building Blocks of Financial Sector Reforms in India and China

The main rationale for monetary management and banking sector reforms in both India and China during 1991-96 underscored the point that the spirit of competitive efficiency emerging in the real sector of a "market-friendly" economy should cover the banking sector also. It is now increasingly felt that the financial sector, including the banking sector, will be able to undertake the task of achieving competitive efficiency only if the system is functioning in a healthy and profitable manner and to become profitable and healthy it will require a considerable measure of operational flexibility and functional autonomy.

Let us now analyse each of the above mentioned building blocks for achieving liberalisation of the financial *cum* banking sector. Competitive efficiency is as important in the operations of the financial sector as it is in the real sector. It gives the saver and investor wide-enough range of choice with regard to both institutions and instruments of finance. In fact, competitive efficiency constitutes the first main building block for financial liberalisation.

Let us now see what India has done to achieve competitive efficiency in the banking sector. The Narasimham Committee recommended in late 1991 the gradual relaxation of the structure of administered interest rates. The RBI has made substantial progress with the job of freeing interest rates with the aim of reflecting emerging market conditions. Further, the Narasimham Committee' emphatically pointed out that there should be no bar to the setting up of new private sector banks provided they conform to the start-up of capital and other requirements. The newly set up private sector bank like UTI Bank and HDFC Bank strongly competing with big public sector banks and are trying to score on the points of operational efficiency better service and maximisation of profits.

The policy with regard to allowing foreign banks to open offices in India has been appreciable liberalised by the Narasimham Committee. Joint ventures between foreign banks and Indian banks started operations during the reform period and they are concentrating on special types of financial services like merchant banking leasing etc. The Committee also wanted that all banks should go for fully computerised systems and produce transparent balance sheets. Fully computerised bank branches are functioning well in major cities and the RBI is continuously insisting that the balance sheets of banks should be as transparent as possible. India has made some progress in the sphere the competitive efficiency but much remains to be done.

China's case on the score competitive efficiency is rather pathetic. Banking sector reforms, as we have seen, came in China as late as 1984 when the PBC (the Central Bank) together with four state-owned specialised commercial banks started functioning in right earnest. Between 1984 and 1989 ten more local area banks with their network of branches were providing direct finance to TVEs and there was semblance of competition. During the second half of the 1980s, a flourshing network of Non-Bank Financial Institution (NBFIS) emerged. Since 1990, the Local Area Banks and NBFIs are competing with the State-owned Banks.

After the passing of the Commercial Bank Laws, 1995, and other key legislations covering the NBFIs, the privately managed banks and financial institution are enjoying more freedom in their operations. Since 1992, Foreign Banks have been allowed to operate in SEZs. Most of the renowned Foreign Banks have now branches in Shanghai and Shenzhen. Of course, work culture among the Chinese banking staff even in the big financial centres, located in SEZs, is fairly satisfactory but is not achieved good as in Taiwan and Singapore. Thus the financial sector reforms, based on competitive efficiency, has not achieved good amount of success in China. First, because it was limited to a few selective spots and, secondly, due to the fact that Chinese Government did not favour a full-fledged policy of encouraging free entry of Private and Foreign Banks even in a liberalised scenario.

The second building block of liberalisation of the financial sector emphasises the point that to perform its task well, the financial system, including the banks, would operate in a healthy manner and earn as much profit as possible. In the Indian case, in accordance with the recommendations of the Narashimham Committee, special Tribunals have been set up during the reform period for tackling the problems of bad and doubtful debts. Inadequacy of capital relative to the scale of risk exposure has been internationally acknowledge as a major problem affecting the health of the banks. As a result, in 1988 the Basle Committee established a norm that capital of a bank must at least be equal to 8 percent of the risk weighted assets. In India during the reform period the capital adequacy norm has been attained by all foreign banks and most the private and public sector banks. It is pertinent to note here that an Asset Reconstruction Fund (ARF) has been recommended by the Narasimham Committee. If the RBI in consultation with the Government of India ultimately decide to set up the ARF then the bad and doubtful debts of banks can be taken off the balance sheets enabling them to recycle the funds, thus released, into more productive uses. Thus there is a strong trend to make the Indian banks operate in a health and profitable manner.

In the case of China, the State-owned banks work within the orbit of a credit plan and have been mainly used as tools for implementing the Government's financial policies. In fact, no special measures have been taken for improving the health of the banks. As expected the Chinese public sector banks do not aim at profit maximisation. However, the Local Area Banks, which cater to the needs of the TVEs, have lately become profitable propositions. This is because TVEs which contributes about 60 percent to the industrial production in China are viable units and regularly payback bank loans.

The third building block is actually an extension of the first two. To be able to play its role in an effective manner and build up its internal strength by earning more profit, the financial system obviously requires a good measure of operational flexibility. The fourth building block, dealing with autonomy in decision making, is inter-related with the third one. In the Indian case with the RBIs recent measures, like freedom for banks in opening new branches and closing old ones (other than rural branches) are meant for achieving greater degree of operational flexibility. In the credit policy of the RBI announced in April 1997, banks have been allowed to evolve own methods for assessing working capital requirements of borrowers. Banks have also been permitted to extend loans to companies against shares on the basis of independent assessment.

The Narasimham Committee not only hammers at operational flexibility but underscores the print that banks should have autonomy in decision making. Unfortunately, even after six years of economic reforms for liberalisation, the Indian bank Chiefs have to satisfy their twin bosses—the RBI and the Finance Ministry of the Government of India.

In China, economic liberalisation has come before political liberalisaton. Under an overall autocratic set-up banking sector reforms have been selective, slow and gradual. These reforms have not followed a comprehensive blueprint for full-fledged liberalisation. Of course, the foreign banks operating in the financial centres of the coastal regions are being run with some amounts of operational flexibility, but their options are few in a regimental system. The Local Area Banks, tagged to TVEs have lately achieved some degree of operational flexibility. But, as expected, autonomy in decision making is a rare thing in the case of the Chinese banks. This is not all surprising since Indian banks, operating under a democratic set-up, lack autonomy in decision making.

Insurance Sector Reforms and the Unfinished Agenda

In spite of the partial fulfillment of the recommendations of the Narasimham Committee, there is still an unfinished agenda in India which requires immediate attention. In China also the task ahead in the sphere of financial sector reforms are highly challenging. While the Government in China tried to keep a firm grip on financial market development to ensure that the banking sector remains a major vehicle for carrying out its monetary policies, it could not do this in a systematic manner. Financial reforms in China, though pragmatic and impressive for a Communist country, never followed a comprehensive blueprint but instead has been characterised by selectivism and gradualism. As a result there remains many grey areas producing gaps in the reforms system. For instance, the development of stock markets concentrated mainly on two centres-Shanghai and Shenzhen. As noted earlier central bank and commercial bank laws in China were enacted as recently as in 1995, while other key legislations, encompassing the NBFIs, freeing of interest rates and recognition of negotiable instruments are expected to be completed by the end of 1997. This deficiency of a solid legislative underpinning has surely produced an adverse impact on China's financial reforms. Lack of solid legislation has delayed the commercialisation of the Chinese state-owned banks. The continued dependence on the Government and its policies has failed to produce the desired level of financial sophistications needed the desired level of financial sophistications needed during the process of growth under economic reforms. In China, from this point of view, the insurance sector is perhaps the biggest casualty. Though in the financial centres in the coastal regions, the service industries have started growing, there has been no systematic and necessary development of general insurance companies. Of course, there is a state-owned Life Insurance Company which acts as a part of the social insurance package which is available in most socialistic countries. It is to be hoped that with the annexation of Hong Kong with main land China, foreign insurance companies, with their bases in Hong Kong will open new branches in SEZs, of mainland China.

In the case of India, a high-powered Committee, under the Chairmanship of R.N. Malhotra, recommended for the privatisation of the insurance sector, in January 1994. The Malhotra Committee has suggested that foreign insurance companies should be allowed entry in India, but should conduct their business of operating through joint ventures with Indian partners.

The Committee has suggested that the Life Insurance Corporation (LIC) which is currently a statutory corporation, should be converted into a company. The present capital of Rs. 5 crores of LIC should be raised to Rs. 200 crores. The

Government should hold 50 percent and the balance should be held by the public at large.

The General Insurance Company (GIC) should cease to be a holding company of four subsidiary companies. These four companies should thereafter function as independent companies. GIC should operate exclusively as a reinsurance company and its capital should be raised to Rs. 200 crores, 50 percent of which should he held by the Government and the remaining by the public. The Committee has recommended stiff eligibility norms for private sector entry in the insurance business. A minimum paid up capital of Rs.100 crores for a new entrant has been suggested. The promoter's holding in a private insurance company should not exceed 40 percent and should, at no time, be less than 26 percent of the total paid up capital. Further , the committee has suggested that no person other than the promoters should be allowed to hold more than 1 per cent equity.

Though more than three years have elapsed since the Malhotra Committee submitted its report to the Government, very little has been done for opening up of the insurance sector. Instead of inviting private enterprise, both Indian and foreign, to the insurance sector, the Government has set-up and Insurance Regulatory Body which has already started functioning though with in a limited sphere. The 1997-98 Union Budget announced a limited opening up of the health insurance sector to foreign companies. The Government proposes to move necessary amendments to enable GIC to float joint ventures with selected Indian or foreign players in the Health Insurance sector. The Finance Minister in the 1997-98 Union Budget has also proposed to permit Unit Trust of India (UTI) to compete with LIC in the sphere of retirement benefits and other types of pension funds. It is well known that the insurance sector reforms has to keep pace with the banking sector reforms so that the financial sector reforms has synchronised with the real sector reforms. It is somewhat disheartening to note that both in India and China insurance sector reform, which is vital component for lubricating the growth of the service sector, has lagged behind.

Though some progress has been made in the banking

sector in India, the tasks ahead should be listed. First, there should be complete ban on generalised loan waivers. Careful targeting of concessional lending to the real needy is an urgent necessity. It should be remembered that what is important is not the cost of credit but the speed at which credit reaches those who are the most deserving ones.

The second urgent need is the immediate revamping of agricultural credit institution and regional rural banks. As in the case of Bangladesh, "Gramin" experiments, the newly proposed Local Area Banks in India should be owned and operated by NGOs in rural areas. Thirdly, the Asset Reconstruction Fund (ARF), as recommended by the Narasimham Committee, should be created with delay and the Special Banking Tribunals, which have already been established, should be given more powers for speedy disposal of pending cases.

Last, but not the least, there should be substantial strengthening of bank's supervision and monitoring roles. In short, there should be a change in the 'mind set' of the people who run our banks. This, of course, depends on the general improvement of the work-culture of all types of workers. In spite of our best efforts we still have a long list of unfinished agenda in the sphere of financial sector reforms. The unfinished agenda in the case of China is even longer as China is a late starter and has refrained from following a systematic comprehensive blue-print. In both the countries, unless the financial sector reforms are completed, the real sector development will be seriously hampered. However, the task is easier in India than in China since the banking sector in India has gained sufficient momentum for continuing the reforms in a speedy manner.

CONCLUDING REMARKS

China, with land area nearly there times that of India but with population growth rate of 1.4 per cent per annum compared to India's 1.9 per cent per annum highlights a success story for economic reforms. While India achieved 4.8 percent average annual growth rate in terms of GDP between 1991-92 and 1995-96, China achieved a growth rate of 13.3 percent during the same period. China, instead of going for a 'big-bang' policy, opted for an experiment with 'gradualism' based on a selective approach. India, started with a 'big-bang' policy between July and December, 1991, but in subsequent years tilted towards 'gradualism'. China under autocratic rule, achieved economic liberalisation without political liberalisation, India, under democratic Government scored full marks in the case of political liberalisation. But achieved only partial success in the sphere of economic liberalisation. The Indian policy makers, during the last few years of economic reforms were forced to give a 'human face' to the reform process by substantially increasing the expenditure for the social sector to make a frontal attack on poverty and unemployment.

Both India and China undertook financial sector reforms mainly emphasizing banking sector reforms, as a follow-up of the policy of gradual liberalisation. Financial sector reforms have focussed attention on three main areas: 'Institutions, instruments and markets'. In the case of China, the absence of a solid legislative back-up seriously hampered the development of central banking and growth of financial institutions between 1984-1995. Central Banking in China obtained a proper shape towards the end of 1995 when the Chinese Central Banking Law was formally enacted. Looking at India we find that the development of the institution of Central Banking was done in a systematic manner and with easy confidence.

Turning to the evolution and growth of money and capital markets we find that compared to India, China is not only a later starter but the growth process is also slow. While the first stock exchange started in Bombay in 1917, China established the first stock exchange in Shenzhen towards the end of 1986. However the Chinese Government's recognition of Shenzhen and Shanghai Stock Exchanges come in 1990-91.

Looking at monetary and financial instruments we find that in China the lack of nationally integrated inter-bank centres and money markets has seriously affected efforts to achieve the transition from direct to indirect instruments and monetary policy. From 1995 onwards, the Variable Reserve Ratio (VRR) became the main instrument of monetary control in China. In India, with the starting the economic reforms, came the freeing of interest rates from July 1991. Under the Indian liberalised scenario, dominated by competitive market forces, Open Market Operations (OMO) has staged a comeback. However, the Bank Rate weapon and the Selective Credit Control instruments are still important.

The main rationale for monetary management and banking sector reforms in both India and China during 1991-96 emphasised the point that the spirit of competitive efficiency, dominating the real sector of a 'market friendly' economy, should also cover the banking sector.

We undertook a comparative analysis of the success and shortfalls of recent banking sector reforms in both India and China in terms of four basic parameters: competitive efficiency, internal strength and a profitability, operational flexibility and autonomy in decision making. We have found that, during the reform period, the Indian banking system has achieved greater amount of competitive efficiency than the Chinese Banks. This is mainly because of intense competition between Indian Banks and foreign banks for improving customer service. In China, this type of competition is visible only amongst the banks operation in SEZs and also in some of the coastal towns. In India, special policy measures have been taken recently for improving the internal strength and profitability of both public sector and private sector banks. In China, this type of special policy measures for increasing profitability and improving the health of the banking system are conspicuous by their absence. Some amount of operational flexibility has been introduced in recent years for banks operating in regions with high growth potential both in India and China. But, in spite of a liberalised set-up, autonomy in decision making is totally absent in China and somewhat neglected by the authorities in the case of the Indian banking system. In short, banks lacks autonomy in decision-making not only under the autocratic set-up in China, but also under a democratic Government in India.

In spite of a partial fulfillment of the recommendations of Narasimham Committee, set-up financial sector reforms in India, there is still an in finished agenda in India which requires immediate attention. In the case of China financial reforms, though pragmatic and impressive for a Communist country, has not followed a rigid, comprehensive blueprint. Rather, it has been characterised by gradualism and selectivism. There are many grey areas which require immediate attention. The unfinished agenda for further financial reforms both in India and China remains highly challenging.

It is disheartening to note that India has done very little in the sphere of insurance sector reform in spite of a number of positive recommendation of an Export Committee (Malhotra Committee) for opening up of the insurance sector. So far China has also not taken any concrete step for the development and reform of the insurance sector. Thus the lack of proper reforms for the insurance sector is a big gap in the agenda for the reforms process. It has to be remembered that the insurance sector reforms constitute a vital component for the smooth running of an expending service sector that emerges during the reform process.

References

Ahuja, K. (1996), *The Banking Sector: After the Reforms'*, Presidential Address, Seventy-Ninth Annual Conference, Indian Economic Association, Gwalior, India.

Berliner, J. (1993), ' *Perestroika and the Chinese Model'*, (Mimeo), Brandeis University.

Chen, E., T. Wong and P.W. Wong (1991), ' *South China Economic Zone: Its Development and Prospect'*, (mimeo)

Chen, J., and B. Hu (1993), ' *China's Rural Industrial Development and Surplus Labour Transfer'*, Presented at the National Workshop on Rural Industrialisation in Post-Reform China, Beijing.

Dixion, X., and 'Others', (1982)—' *China's Search for Economic Growth: The Chinese Economy Since 1949'*, New World Press, Beijing.

Fairbank, J. (1992), *'China a New History'*, Cambridge, M. A. : Harvard University Press.

Gale Johnson, D. (1990), *'The People's Republic of China: 1978-1990'* ICEG, San Francisco.

Ghosh, A., (1994), *'Economic Reforms in India and China and the Need for Revamping the Banking Sector'*. Artha Beekashana Vol. 3., No. 2, December.

Ghosh, A., (1996), *' Liberalisation Programmes and Structural Adjustment in India'* in Liberalisation, Adjustment and Reforms in India, R.K. Sen (ed). , Bodh Publication, Kanpur (India).

Ghosh, A. (1997), *'Indian Economy: Its Nature and Problem'* 27th Edition, The New Book Stall, Calcutta.

Gupta, S.P., N. Stern and A. Hussain (ed.) (1995), *'Development Patterns and Institutional Structures: China and India'* Allied Publishers Limited, New Delhi.

Hu, J. and M.S. Khan (1997), *'Why is China Growing So Fast?'* IMF, Washington D. C.

Lardy, N., (1989), *'Technical Change and Economic Reform in China: A Tale of Two Sectors'* (mimeo)

McMillan, J. and R. Naughton (1992), *'How to Reform a Planned Economy: Lesson From China'*, Oxford Review of Economic Policy.

Mehran, H. and M. Quintyn (1996), *'Financial Sector Reforms in China'* Finance and Development, Vol. 33, No. 1, March.

Narasimham, M. (1992), *'Report of the Committee on Financial System, 1991'*, Standard Book Company, New Delhi.

Narasimham, M. (1993), *'Financial Sector Reforms: The Unfinished Agenda;* The A.D. Sroff Memorial Trust, Bombay.

Perkins, D. (1992), *'China's "Gradual" Approach to Market Reforms'* (mimeo)

Rangarajan, C. (1995), *' Monetary Management: The Changing Framework' Indian Economic Journal*, Vol. 43, No. 1, July-September.

Rangarajan, C. (1996), *'The Financial Sector Reform—The Next Phase'* Banking Finance, Vol. IX, No. 12, December.

Rawski, T. (1993), *'Progress Without Privatization: The Reforms of China's State Industries'*, (Mimeo).

Reynolds, B. (ed.) (1987), *'Reforms in China: Challenges and Choices'*, Report of the Chinese Economic System Reform Research Institute, New York.

Sachs, J and W.T. Woo (1994), *'Structural Factors in the Economic Reforms of China, Eastern Europe and the Former Soviet Union's Economy Policy* (mimeo).

Srinivasan, T.N. (1994), *'India's Economic Reforms: Tasks Ahead'* ICEG, San Francisco.

Srinivasan, T. N. (1994), *'Agriculture and Trade in China and India* ICEG, San Fransisco.

World Bank (1992), *'China Strategies for Reducing Poverty in the 1990s'*, Washington D.C.

World Bank (1994), *'China—Internal Market Development and Regulation'*, Washington D. C.

World (1996), *India: 'Five Years of Stabilization and Reform and the Challenges Ahead'*, Washington D.C.

APPENDIX

Selected Key Indicators—India and China

Years	*1993-94*		*1994-95*		*1995-96*	
Indicators	*China*	*India*	*China*	*India*	*China*	*India*
GDP Growth Rate	14.1	6.0	14.6	6.9	14.8	7.1
Population Growth Rate	1.5	2.1	1.4	2.0	1.4	1.9
Inflation Rate*	18.0	8.4	160	10.9	13.0	9.7
Lending Rates of Commercial Banks	11.0	14.0	11.5	15.0	12.1	15.5

*Based on WPI.

Sources: (1) Statistical Outline of India, 1996-97, Tata Publications.
(2) Econmic Survey, 1996-97, Govt. of India.
(3) World Bank (1994), 'China—Internal Market Development and Regulation', Washington D.C.
(4) World Bank (1996), 'India: Five Years of Stabilization and Reform and the Challenges Ahead', Washington, D.C.

CHAPTER

6

Whither Corruption in Independent India

D.L. NARAYANA

INTRODUCTION

1997 is the Golden Jubilee year of India's Independence. The British transferred power on 15th August 1947 to India which completes fifty years of democratic rule by 15th August 1997. The British who came to India as traders embarked on the conquest of India that commenced with the Battle of Plassey 1757. Robert Clive's army of 800 Englishmen, 2200 Indian mercenaries routed a large force of 50,000 soldiers of the Bengal Nawab on the paddy fields of Plassey to herald British rule that last for about two centuries. According to K.M. Panikkar,[1] the Battle of Plassey was "not a battle, but a transaction between stock brokers in which the office of Nawab was sold to the East India Company. The skirmish was more significant for its political and shady financial implications rather than the military consequences. The first century of British rule from 1957 to 1857 of India was marked by plunder that supplied much required capital for investment for the acceleration of Industrial Revolution in England which further enhanced the colonial domination of the Indian economy.

The growth of national movement since the Sepoy Mutiny of 1857, which was the first national freedom struggle, advanced by the National Congress and the Quit India Movement of 1942 during the Second World War time started by Mahatma Gandhi weakened the foundations of British rule in India. Great Britain was forced to concede the Indian demand for Independence. When the eventual exists could not be postponed, the British resorted to their game of divide and rule. Churchill's statement on transfer of power was an index of the mind set of the Englishmen, that the British were transferring power to "men of straw whose trace will not remain after a few years". But the approach of the day of transfer of power made many Englishmen lament the loss of the brightest jewel, the Indian empire. The withdrawal on 15th August 1947 was the greatest disengagement in History. The 1997 withdrawal of the British from Hong Kong brought its empire to an end. Imperialist rule, "government of other people by other people, and for other people" cannot survive for all times.

THE ACHIEVEMENTS OF FREE INDIA

The Fifty years of democratic rule of India has completely falsified Churchill's prognosis. The quality of leadership at national and state level seasoned in the freedom struggle attained the calibre, character and commitment, is next to none in the World. Despite the innumerable problems of transition from colonial status to the status of a free country and the atmosphere fraught with tensions, intrigue, jealousy and hostility, India withstood the shock of the assassination of Mahatma Gandhi, the Father of the Nation and successfully tackled the stupendous challenge of migration and settlement of Ten million refugees in the wake of vivi- section of India in record time. It constitute the biggest operation of human history. India drafted and adopted a democratic constitution which is by all means one of the best in the world. Moreover, India heroically defended the country in the wars unleased by China (1962) and Pakistan

(1964 and 1971). India provided sound leadership to the non-aligned nations and emerged as a good balancing force in the world fraught with super-power rivalries.

India launched planned economic development and achieved a linear growth rate of 3.5 percent, with higher growth in recent years as against 0.75 to 1.0 percent of growth rate from 1900 to 1950 under the British rule. The country eliminated famines and achieved self-sufficiency in foodgrain production. It obviated the pitiable problem of living "from ship to mouth". Although the five year plans aimed at raising the standard of living of the growing population, limited success was achieved on account of population explosion from 350 million in 1947 to about 950 million today. While poverty is not eliminated completely, considerable proportion of the population about 36 percent (1993) is still below poverty line. Population explosion neutralised the gains of economic development considerably in terms of increasing unemployment and under-employment, apart from the less effective utilisation of outlays in the different sectors of the economy resulting in rising prices of commodities. The number of people living below poverty line in absolute terms shows no sign of significant decrease in relation to India's population on the eve of Independence. Another problem of importance is that India is caught up in a debt trap involving interest payments of about Rs.60,000 crores. As both external and internal debts are rising significantly now the Jubilee year of Independence is caught up in a serious dept trap. India has emerged as an Asian tiger in population explosion unlike the established Asian tigers in economic growth like Japan, Hong Kong, Singapore, Taiwan South Korea, Indonesia, Malaysia, Thailand and even China. These are also known as the newly industrialising countries. Despite some limitations, India has acquitted as the largest democratic country in the World today.

THE INCIDENCE OF CORRUPTION AMONG DIFFERENT COUNTRIES

Independence is not license from all restraint and self-discipline. According to Gandhiji, Swaraj was the prime goal of free India. Swaraj is self-rule and disciplined rule from within. Swaraj was not merely freedom from foreign rule. It is much more than freedom to every Indian as individual, freedom to all from poverty, pestilence, persecution and extortion. Above all good governance and proper enforcement of law and order. Most important is corruption-free administration and immaculate probity in public life. In fine, Swaraj is the pathway to comprehensive Swaraj.

The session for the peaceful transfer of power from Britain to India at the mid-night hour of August 14-15, 1947 concluded with the remarkable speech and prophetic warning of Philosopher Statesman, Dr. S. Radhakrishnan on the eve of the ushering in free India.

"Our opportunities are great but let me warn you that when power outstrips ability, we will fall on evil days. We should develop competence and ability which would help us to utilise opportunities which are now open to us. From tomorrow morning from mid-night today—we cannot throw the blame on the Britisher. We have to assume the responsibility ourselves. A free India will be judged by the way in which it will serve the interests of the common man in the matter of food, clothing, shelter and social activities". "Unless we destroy corruption in high places, love of power, profiteering and black-marketing . . . we will not be able to raise the standards of efficiency in administration as well as in the production and distribution of the necessary goods of life". This warning given half a century ago has come true.

Corruption in India is not of recent origin. Indian History reveals that the conquest of India by the British has been the 27th invasion which bristled with corruption during its rule from a far off place. Twenty-five centuries ago Kautilya's Arthasastra categorised 40 different ways in which the King's cronies use to defraud the State of its revenues. Today there may be thousands of ways through which corruption is taking place in Government, Public Sector, Private Sector, Educational Sector, Rural Sector or any other sector where there is scope for embezzlement of funds. The Golden Jubilee Year of Independence of India has earned the dubious distinction of being a rich and expanding mine of scams. The list has grown over the years with Rs. 9000 crores securities scam, the Indian Bank scam worth Rs. 1200 crores, Rs. 950 crores Bihar Fodder scam, Rs. 200 crores Bihar bitumen scam, Rs. 133 crores Urea scam, Rs. 58 crores CRB scam, the multi-core Hawala scam and the telecom scam. The contemporary trend in India is the emergence of politicians, public men, businessmen and bureaucrats as corruption kings. There are several small and big scams waiting to explode, if there were to be access to people to information about public dealings and transactions. Indeed several rural development scams are waiting to be unearthed but for the tactical bureaucratic delays in bringing out such issues.

Gunnar Myrdal known as Adam Smith of poverty of Nations made an exciting statement in his book "The Challenge of World Poverty", "one of the most flagrant examples of bias in the post war approach is the virtual taboo against including the important facts of corruption in the analysis of development problems of under developed countries—It is possible to read hundreds of books and articles on under development and development without even encountering the word Corrupton."[2] Even Western economists use to keep silence on the issue and at times erroneous thoughts are put forward "that bribery is a necessary and not harmful lubricant for a cumbersome administration", while the truth is that corruption is one of the causes of administration becoming cumbersome" as asserted by Gunnar Myrdal.[3]

S. Rajaratnam, Minister of Foreign Affairs and Labour in his bold address entitled "Bureaucracy and Kleptocracy" to the union leaders of public servants in Asia, criticised the taboo held by most economists against discussion of Corruption". "It is amazing how otherwise excellent studies on development problems in Asia and Africa avoid any serious reference to the fact of corruption. It is not that writers do not know of its existence but its relevance to the question of political stability and rapid economic development appears not to have been fully appreciated. It may also be that a serious problem of the subject has been avoided lest it should offend the sensibilities of Asian."[4] What is more alarming is the argument that bribery bureaucracies promote bureaucratic efficiency, innovation and rapid economic development in developing countries. But there is no convincing evidence according to S. Rajaratnam, that corruption assisted economic development or strengthened political stability as the minister emphasized. He further stressed that "Kleptocracy will steer itself, whether those in power want it or not, into more and more corruption and finally into economic and political chaos. This has been the life cycle of societies in Asia during that last two decades."[5] Gunnar Myrdal expressed that racial inferiority and southern idleness may not be admissible facts nevertheless productivity in under-developed countries may well be lessened by low living standards and climatic conditions. Traditional institutions and attitudes and widespread corruption are other facts which cannot be politely ignored in framing plans. Indeed the contemporary level of corruption in India is an important constraint for the percolation of economic growth for advancing social development. Corruption is most conspicuous while the percolation impact of economic growth is least visible. As a matter of fact it is easier to get blood from a stone than getting a formal signature from a revenue office without speed money which is getting enhanced regularly.

As a matter of fact corruption is so widespread in India today that the entire political system from the city centres to remote villages is floating on unaccounted money requiring attention and action without further delay. A person who enriches himself with political power and economic power through illicit transactions commands respect and public esteem in any walk of life. He develops following as he is capable of disbursing benefits or helping through recommendations. Political clout matters much in the society as the leaders influence decision-making at different levels in the Government sector and also in private sector. A person who discharges duties with principles ordained by his position does not enjoy superiority. The ethical difference between the corrupt and the non-corrupt is eroding day-by-day. The corrupt are having higher vertical mobility and prosperity in society as compared to their peers. Persons known fro established integrity and efficiency are elbowed out of deserving position and power as they do not fit into the culture of authorities practicing parallel economy. They are becoming victims of stagnation and frustration.

The politics, controversies, CBI enquiries, court cases, Statewide "Bandh", other consequences and abysmal fall in ethical values of the Bihar fodder scam has no parallel in the history of black economy. This deteriorating crisis in values is a matter of greater concern and alarm than ever before in the history of India. It is a matter of surmise whether the rate of exploitation involved in the prevailing corruption practices in India today is more than the exploitation of India by the foreign rule during the colonial era.

Corruption has become an established way of life. As the corrupt are more prosperous, the activity is quite attractive for practising when opportunity arises. For analytical purposes, different levels of corruption are distinguished. Grass eating is the collection of small amounts in offices by lower cadre of employees, which may not be a burden even to the payers. Meat eating is the practice of fixing the collection of specified amounts of money for the approval and allotment of each activity. Institution eating is the spread of corruption among the members of the organization involving heavy amounts of money that influences the quality and cost of the work. When it spreads across the length and breadth of the State. It amounts to state eating. When it covers all states, it becomes nation eating. The Bihar fodder scam is not a case of grass-eating, it is a case of State eating. What is still more significant is that the Bihar fodder scam is an outstanding index of the poor quality of financial control that is now prevailing among some of the state Governments in India. Indeed "the fodder scam is but the small symptom of a deep and chronic malady afflicting the Bihar Government and quite a few other state governments as well. Basic financial control has collapsed; audit and accounts are in wild disorder and the constitutional arrangements for legislative control over government finances have completely broken down".[6]

As compared to the legitimate aspirations of independence, the available scientific evaluation of the incidence of corruption among the different countries reveals that India is drifting very badly with alarming incidence of corruption. The Transperancy International[7] (TI) is a multi-national organisation started by Peter Eigen dedicated to curb corruption in international business. It was launched to assess the degree to which public officials and politicians in particular countries accept bribes. It makes an assessment of illicit payments in public procurement and embezzling of public funds. It defined corruption as the "misuse" of public power and assets for private gain. Its headquarters in Berlin. According to TI's corruption Index of 1996, developing countries emerge as the most corrupt areas, Nigeria blazing the trail followed by Pakistan, Kenya, Bangladesh and China ranking fifth. The least corrupt countries with first rank are New Zealand, Denmark, Sweden and Finland with cleanest administration. Singapore gets seventh rank as the least corrupt area in Asia.

Corruption is a global phenomenon. The ranks with high corruption are :

12th rank - Britain
13th rank - Germany
14th rank - U.S.A.
17th rank - Japan
19th Rank - France
32nd rank - Spain
34th rank - Italy: Most Corrupt in Europe
46th rank - India

The TI ranked countries by their corruption based on Survey by risk analysts and businessmen. It practices quiet diplomacy without exposing reports on bribery. The organisation has acquired international recognition. It is argued that TI survey may reveal some bias in favour of western industrial nations, for the recipients of bribes are officials in developing countries, the payers are mostly companies in developed countries, who normally use intermediaries or agents in developing countries to pay bribes to secure business and favours. In the universal language all corruption amounts to graft, bribery and pay offs which are variously called, "bakshish" in the Arab world, "dash" in Africa, "hawala" in India, "mafia" in Russia and Italy. It is not clear from the TI survey data whether it has taken into account the rampant administrative corruption that prevails in India in the execution of different plan schemes at various levels including the villages. Comparable data of the incidence of corruption as a ratio of GDP for the different countries is not available. Probably it may give a more valuable comparison to prepare action programmes, if the Governments are interested.

CORRUPTION IN THE POVERTY ALLEVIATION SCHEMES

Dr. John Echeverri Gent[8] has made a detailed study of the implementation of rural poverty alleviation programmes in Maharashtra and West Bengal. He is quite aware of the hypothesis that the rural structure in India characterised by extreme inequalities of land and other assets as a formidable obstacle to the success of poverty alleviation programmes. Political power represented by the coalition of landed interests, politicians and Government officials can be a formidable obstacle to equitable rural development. But he is quite confident that the obstacle can be overcome in a number of ways. He found that when Jawahar Rozgar Yojana (JRY) and Employment Guarantee Scheme (EGS) produced assets benefiting the poor, enhanced their welfare and facilitated a qualitative change in their status. The well-organised rural poor with improved consciousness of their rights are emerging as counter-vialing power to reckon with, and their impact on implementing authorities was often quite decisive. Innovative and imaginative public policy can also effectively defeat the machinations of the vested interests. The Prime obstacle for effective implementation of the poverty alleviation programmes, either JRY or EGS known as Employment Assurance Scheme and the MPs Local Area Development Scheme started in 1993, the centrally funded programmes is due to rampant corruption which is a powerful weapon used by the rich to defeat the defraud the poor. The most effective way of checking corruption according to Dr. John Echeverri-Gent is to enhance the accountability of implementing authority by providing the public with the opportunity to monitor their conduct. It is to be noted that at the level of local government, Panchayat officials are able to conceal from the public their use of JRY funds to advance their private interests. The best way of tackling this problem is to ensure the transperancy of panchayat institutions.

Echeverri Gent is quite optimistic about the possibility of promoting equitable rural development without radical structural reforms. Poverty alleviation programmes can overcome the constraints presented by rigid social structure and facilitate equitable rural development through of right policies and strategies. Indira Hiraway [9] and Piet Terhal made a study of Indian and International experiences in rural and public works programmes which are largely aimed at providing work and wages for the rural poor in the event of emergencies or when there is a situation of acute unemployment and poverty. The programmes could also help to create infrastructural assets like roads, irrigation facilities, schools, etc., and contribute towards appropriate environmental management by watershed development and afforstation through labour intensive techniques. The basic idea of intensive utilisation of the rural unemployment through appropriate schemes is a very sound method of advancing rural welfare. But the studies reveal that the excellent idea is not easily translated into action and achievement.

The Implementation of the programmes bristles with a number of problems. The programmes are often introduced on *adhoc* basis without a long-term policy framework. Lack of political commitment is another limitation. Misuse of the funds allotted for the programmes (such as National Rural Employment Programme, Rural Landless Employment Guarantee Programme and Jawahar Rozgar Yojana) by lower level politicians and bureaucrats is a great stumbling block for the progress of rural schemes. The authors confess that the overall picture emerging from case studies cannot be described as every encouraging, "none of the programmes can be rated as highly successful and when there were successful, it was only for relatively short periods". The studies postulate that such rural works may not be useful as a long-term strategy. However the authors conclude that the Maharashtra Employment Guarantee Scheme was able to achieve a measure of success in alleviating poverty. They felt that a Maharashtra type of employment guarantee scheme can be made to work in India as a whole with suitable modifications. According to the authors, Chinese experience was most successful. The relative superiority of the Chinese model is traced to the repression of freedom to a considerable extent. Anjali Bagwe[10] surveyed the role of status of women at Masura, a large coastal village in South Maharashatra. The author's grassroot level research work went on over 12 years. She covered the various facets of rural life in a detailed way. The study brings home the stark reality that the governmental welfare schemes have in many instances simply failed to reach the intended beneficiaries. The author laments that many development schemes are clearly manipulated to fill the coffers of local politicians.

The three evaluation studies confirm that the rampant corruption is standing in the way of achieving the expected results under the poverty alleviation programmes in the villages. The funds allotted to the schemes are enriching politicians and the Government agencies. According to the former Prime Minister, Rajiv Gandhi, 85 percent of the funds for anti-poverty Programmes were diverted before reaching the beneficiaries who got access only for 15 percent of the funds allotted. The two lessons of the above studies are: (1) the enhancement of the accountability of the implementing authorities with the organisation of the rural poor as a counter-vialing power, and (2) Utilisation of the Maharashtra model of employment guarantee scheme with suitable modifications for India as a whole for satisfactory results.

BUREAUCRACY AND CORRUPTION

Right to information to citizens is an essential requisite to undermine and arrest the practice of corruption by the bureaucrats and the legislators. According to Arun Roy, an I.A.S., Officer, who resigned from the cadre in 1975, "The system was so soaked in corruption that fighting it being a part of it was just impossible. Either you become a cog in the wheel of bureaucracy and remain detached from the needs of the people, whom you are supported to serve, or dissociate yourself and demand your right as an ordinary citizen."[11] She postulated that "in a democracy, secrecy will not serve any purpose but only breed corruption and give rise to more scams. Essentially the bureaucrats and legislators will have to shed their shackling mindsets and people have to release that ills of liberty can be overcome by being more liberal".[12] To be able to unmask corrupt officials and force them to return the siphoned off money to jeering members of public may be counted as a measure of success. Bureaucratic integrity and political will are buzzwords. More important than the number of frauds exposed, people should be in a position to make a difference in their living by exercising their right to question and auditing public expenses.

If the legislation on right to information comes through, it will undoubtedly sow the needs of a long overdue social revolution. The debates among the intelligentsia advocated the right to freedom of speech and expression. Now the idea is spreading for the economic well-being of the people, as everybody realises, the right to information springs from concerns of survival. The right to information raises the hope for ethical governance. Legislation to provide the right to information exists in a number of developed countries. Sweden has 200 years old law for that purpose. The U.S. implemented its Freedom of Information Act in 1966, Australia and New Zealand in 1982 and Canada in 1983. India has to pass appropriate legislation to facilitate the right to information as early as possible. Pending legislation non-governmental organisations and public workers may strive for the right of information on payment they may demand photocopy of documents relating to the developmental projects at the block level to check the malpractice. Social auditing gains importance as a check against corrupt practices. The Mazdoor Kisan Shakti Sangathan has been waging a long struggle for people's access to the accounts and related papers at the level of local government in the State of Rajasthan. The Rajasthan Government after having agreed to allow the people's access to such information, is now going back on its word.[13]

HUMAN DEVELOPMENT WITH VALUES

According to the Fourth Human Development Report of

UNDP, India ranks among the least development countries in the world with its rank of 136 out of 173 countries. Canada is at the top, along with Switzerland, Japan, Sweden and Norway. Social development in India is at a very low level according to the Human Development Index of 0.293 of India as against 0.612 of China and 0.651 of Sri Lanka as per H.D. Report of 1992. India's HDS rank has 121 as against 79 of China and 76 of Sri Lanka.

Its adult literacy is 48.2 percent as against 73 percent of China and 88.4 per cent of Sri Lanka. Adult female literacy is 34 percent as against 62 per cent of China and 84 percent of Sri Lanka. Life expectancy in India is 59.1 years as against 70.1 of China and 70.9 of Sri Lanka.

In the worlds of Frederick Harbison,[14] "Human resources constitute the ultimate basis for the wealth of nations. Capital and material resources are passive factors of production; human beings are the active agents who accumulate capital, exploit natural resources, build social, economic and political organizations, and carry forward national development. Clearly a country which is unable to develop skills and knowledge of its people and to utilise them effectively in the national economy will be unable to develop anything else". Not only knowledge and skills determine the quality and calibre of human resources, but also the values animating the human resources go a long way of determine individual efficiency at micro and macro levels. Right values maximise the contribution of human factor to output and economic growth.

Rampant corruption in a country implies the functioning of social order without normal human values, such as truth, justice, love, peace and non-violence. Righteous behaviour on the part of individual warrants the pursuit of normal human values conductive for the success of democracy. Misuse of power with greed for material culture account for rampant corruption. It is well surmised that there is no country in the world where politics attracts the interest of the people more than in India. According to B.K. Nehru[15], "the proportion of criminals and history-sheeters in the Legislative Assemblies of the country has been increasing from election to election". Indeed the U.P Legislature at one time had 53 persons involved in attempts to murder and several confirmed criminals.

Justice is a very wide concept. It encompasses the whole range of morality, virtue, righteousness, respect for human life, compassion and rule of law. There is a saying that man's capacity for justice makes democracy possible, while man's propensity for injustice makes democracy necessary.[16] In a country where corruption is rampant, judiciary activism has to play vital role to curb the proliferation of scams, big or small as the case may be. No source of power or influence shall deter the judiciary from discharging its sacred duty to the society in assessing the criminals and awarding deterrent punishments.

India ranks third in the availability of skilled manpower in the world. The main function of education is to humanise people and facilitate the development of corporate culture for sustaining the regular functioning of democracy. An effective educational system aims at enlightening the minds and illuminating the hearts of the student population. What is now happening in the country is educating the heads to utilse their hands without any visible good impact on the hearts. Consequently the human resources are better in their professions as compared to their contribution to social solidarity and corporate culture. India is imploding not only as the second most populous country in the world but also with vast social differentiation on account of its most heterogeneous social composition with about four thousand castes and sub-castes, four hundred languages and about ten religions differentiation impinging on social cohesion and corporate spirit.

Free India is witnessing today rampant communal struggle, caste struggle and regional struggle within States cutting at the root of cooperative human spirit required for better social and economic development. For instance, not only castes, but a multiplicity of sub-castes are flying at each others' throat—Yadavas against Thakuras, Marathas against Chitpavans, Patels against Desais, Reddis against Kammas, Vakkaligas against Lingayats, Thevars against Harijans, apart from one set of

Brahmins against another, as also Harijans *versus* caste Hindus and Madigas *versus* Malas. The widespread caste struggle along with class struggle, not to speak of communal struggle are undermining healthy human spirit required for socio-economic development. Rampant corruption and crisis in character have robbed polity of all values, truth and righteousness. *Satyameva Jayathe* has become a mockery. Revolution in political culture is a crucial requisite for arresting the contemporary social crisis in character to pave the way for better social environment, advancement and economic development. With a population nearing one billion constituting one-sixth of World population, India has not been a position to achieve national solidarity in spite of its progress as an independent nation over the five decades. While India a free from Chaos, its nationhood is still incomplete and its role in international affairs is not significant.

MANAGEMENT OF UNIVERSITIES

Higher education experienced phenomenal growth for the development of human resources since Independence. Against 25 Universities, 700 colleges with 2.66 lakhs students, India to-day has about 200 Universities, over 8000 colleges with 50 lakhs students. The importance of University education needs no assertion. The Report of the Indian Education Commission, 1961-65, rightly summed up. "The destiny of India is now being shaped in the class rooms. This we believe, is no rhetoric. It is education that determines the level of prosperity, welfare and security of the people". Academic profession is the mother of all professions.

While the University education has achieved tremendous quantitative growth, the qualitative deterioration in the standards of trained human resources is abnormal and abominable. The number of effective working days of the universities are regularly declining. It is a matter of doubt whether any University is working for 180 working days, the requisite optimum standard. Post-graduates who come out of the Universities by indulging in malpractices and short cuts are the promoters of non-work culture disturbing the social equilibrium. Universities are reduced a feuding political camps with a career politics, supplanting scholarship without making sincere attempts to salvage the sinking temples. University administrators who give great priority for making money are completely neglecting the management of Universities to advance the education goals. Student indiscipline is rampant. The prime cause for the disastrous deterioration in the management of universities is traced to politicisation in the appointment of vice-chancellors. A Vice-Chancellor makes or mars a Universities depending on his calibre commitment, and professional excellence. The collusion between teacher politicians and the public leaders is avoiding the appointment of right and competent academicians as Vice-Chancellors. Bad coins are driving away the good coins. Gresham's law is operating vigorously in the appointment of vice-chancellors. Populist appointments governed by vested interest account for substantial deterioration of the management of Universities during the last two decades. Some Universities experienced significant scams, sale of University properties for personal gain and absolute negligence of educational management.

According to the Amrik Singh Committee Report on the working of Universities in Andhra Pradesh, the most urgent task is that Universities working needs to be "decisively depoliticised. This would mean appointing the right kind of Vice-Chancellors, nominating suitable persons to various University bodies, doing so on time giving due representation to different interest and different points of view". The Committee made about 70 recommendations for improving the universities in the state. The Committee also felt that the report will be of great significance for a better functioning of universities in the country. But the report is in cold storage.

METAMORPHOSIS OF SOCIAL TRENDS

J.K. Galbraith comprehended democracy in India as a functional anarchy. Social scene in India is characterised by corruption, commercialisation of political life, criminalisation of politics, casteism, communalism and regionalism with deleterious consequences for national integration and formation of stable Central Government under single party majority or a few parties.

The country is experiencing an intractable crisis of deteriorating values landing in moral crisis of ethical values in the pursuit of economic, political and social activities. Although India is working democracy with a federal structure, its current social trends signify social indiscipline that is not conductive to rapid development.

Social problems may be micro in character. Macro problems tend to be dominant in a society. If a problem is of normal or optimum nature, it may not be case for alarm or serious action. For instance, if the temperature of a man is 98.4 degree Farhenheit, the person is healthy, if it is 100, a matter of consideration, 105 a source of anxiety, 110 many mean catastrophe. As noted earlier corruption is a global phenomenon. If its incidence is minimal in a country, it may not be deleterious either to society or the economy. When it becomes stupendous or prodigious, it may precipitate social, political and economic instability in the country. Italy has experienced the largest number of Government changes in the past-war period on account of problems arising out of corruption. In a similar way when the gravity of social problems is alarming, they necessitate appropriate social action either by Government of public interference or private action to control them. They may necessitate concerted social action. An attempt is made to analyse the different social trends in India that determine social efficiency either directly or indirectly. The formulation of trends with their qualitative character reveals the seriousness of the issues.

If the social trends emerge as evils social efficiency gets aggregated deepening the social crisis. The following are some of the social trends.

1. Politics without principles;
2. Democracy without discipline;
3. Wealth without work;
4. Commerce without ethics;
5. Knowledge without character;
6. Education without merit;
7. Science without humanity;

8. Worship without sacrifice;
9. Pleasure without conscience;
10. Rights without duties;
11. Administration without accountability;
12. Power without responsibility;
13. Social order without normal moral fabric;
14. Social chaos without political perception;
15. Rampant corruption without control;
16. Increasing tax evasion without limit;
17. Increasing accumulation of black money that is threatening the normal working of the economy;
18. Democracy without a functional bureaucracy;
19. Corporate practices without ethical values;
20. Political and commercial nexus without ethical basis;
21. Increasing pressure of private corporate sector for tax incentives;
22. Audit reports without adequate response and responsibility from State Government and also Central Government;
23. Government without effective law and order;
24. Government without required stability;
25. Government without solidarity of the political parties;
26. Power corrupts, fear of losing power corrupts more;
27. Corruption trends to be follow without exposure;
28. Democracy without discipline the functional efficiency;
29. Democracy cannot be sustained without responsibility;
30. Governance without vibrant discourse and discussion undermines the capacity for democracy;
31. Grab-as-much-as you can syndrome accounts for the governing bodies without the exercise of vibrant discourse;
32. Elimination of MLAs and MPs from the scope of prevention of Corruption Act will aggravate the parallel economy;
33. People's representatives at different levels are

indulging in self service than in social service;

34. Denigrating Mahatma Gandhi as Father of Nation by indulging in rival names exposes political bankruptcy on account of greed for power and riches;
35. Total prohibition in any country or region never attained success;
36. Indian Solidarity and nationhood is not complete in spite of fifty years of Independence;
37. Evolving social anarchy abandons the future of a nation to chance;
38. Without rural development, there is no national development in a country of villages;
39. As our cities are turning into urban nightmares with many people in too little space, there is a need for a promotion of balanced urbanization, in particular the control of mega cities;
40. The philosophy of Janmabhoomi Development is a real Gandhian principle translated in India as Community Development Programme. The Kothari Commission visualised it as a desirable policy to introduce work experience to the students in the universities. Janmabhoomi Development Programme may be made a regular feature of colleges and universities and similar institutions;
41. The functioning of democracy bristles with a number of distortions. Political power has become an end in itself. Political leaders are practising every possible means to win an election to occupy positions in Government. The electoral process has been corrupted as political parties, groups and leaders are spending lakhs of rupees to win an election by buying and bribing voters and their local leaders who are influential to mobilise votes. If the power of money proves inefficient to win over the electoral support of voters, professional criminals are openly employed by political leaders or terrorise the non-responding voters or sections of society. Politicians are employing "illegitimate and illegal" methods for winning elections. This growing criminalisation of politics in

India is having adverse impact on democratic governance and the public services at different levels. If criminals occupy seats of power in Assemblies, Lok Sabha and Council of Ministers, it opens up the floodgates of illegal culture with disastrous impact on society. As the elections are involving heavy expenditure, the elected representatives begin to mobilise the collect funds by utilising every iota of their influence and power. Government funding of parliament and State Legislative elections may go a long way to cut the vicious circle of parallel economy and lay a foundation for a clean society, as the vicious circle of mobilisation of funds from all possible sources commences with elections. The peoples' representatives try to help their financiers. Again they look forward for mobilising finances for the next elections. Thus, fund collection becomes a vicious culture.

42. Politics has become a visible profession in the country. Peoples' representatives at different levels are more concerned with feathering their nests than learning from society to advance social interests to strengthen the democracy through effective discussions. If this trend is not reversed, the very basis of democratic self-government-based on rule of law may dwindle and disappear. The only hope for India's near billion people possessing a store of talent may muddle through a survival technique in spite of their drift into non-goverance in the face of different types of struggles and problems. Its centuries old history reveals a capacity for social and political discourse, which is very much complicated now on account of its most heterogeneous social composition with a vast population.

Healthy corporate spirit among the people will be a strong foundation for democracy. The need of the hour is healthy human spirit in its different ramifications to arrest the deepening and widening the social crisis in character;

43. The MPLDA Scheme providing Rs.1 crore for each parliamentary constituency as a catalyst of local development is an ill-conceived and unhealthy measure as its impact on a few preferred pockets divides the political base of the MP. The pressure of MPs for top-most priority in executing the scheme in preferred areas is increasing the apathy of District Officials. It is also a preposterous democratic measure under the contemporary social environment of scams. The demand for funding may go on increasing. It may result in creating a rival agency in the constituency as against the official administration. Constituency development fund either at parliament level or at the State Legislature Level is an ill-conceived concept.
44. Ever increasing "Bandhs" and "Dharanas" without rule and rhyme are disturbing and dislocating civic life involving violence, deaths and loss of property. While banning them may be deemed undemocratic, some rational legal restraint has to be imposed to lessen the turmoil. The culprits indulging in destructive activity have to be death with seriously without mercy.
45. As regards the safety and security of the nation, the policy that defense is more important than opulence holds good. Accordingly the Government has to evolve the priorities of defence expenditure under the plan programmes.
46. Although most of Asian and African countries secured freedom from colonial rule five decades ago, most of them except for about four countries, are still wallowing in poverty. Catherine Caufield's thought-provoking study" The World Bank and the Poverty of Nations" throws valuable light of the problem. She aptly stated, "Given the fact that development funds, including the World Bank's are ultimately supplied by the ordinary tax-payers in the donor nations, there is much truth in the saying that development—at least in the monopolistic formulatic,

> foreign-dominated, argonaut, and failed from that we have known—is largely a matter of poor countries"[17] Development financing is perpetuating a cruel joke on the poor countries as can be seen from the outflow of loan repayments far exceeding the loan inflows. In 1994 the developing world received $ 167.8 billion in foreign loan and paid $ 169.5 billion in debt service—a net transfer from the poor to the rich of $1.7 billions. She analysed the several cases of bad loan management. She highlighted the force to which aid financing has been reduced. What makes the scene worse is that foreign aid is becoming a "habit forming drug". If so, how can the poor countries can help themselves, if after a half century of loan financing, they become poorer?

The divesting criticism of Catherine Caufield finds ample corroboration in the study of the problem by Teresa Hayter who made a detailed study of the financing by World Bank which financed the study. Appalled by the contents of the book, the World Bank refused to publish the study. Later it was published in England by Penguin under the title "Aid as Imperialism", which is an indictment of the programmes of the World Bank financing the developing countries. Catherine Caufield's study has successfully established the truth that billions of dollars which the World Bank poured did not make any dent world's poverty. "The Assault on Poverty" Advocated by Robert McNamara, President, World Bank, during 1970s with great emphasis has become hallow and a dismal failure.

The World Bank's loan operations over the decades failed to alleviate the incidence of poverty in the developing countries as the recent studies have revealed. Arun Ghosh [18] has expressed alarming pessimism about the pursuit of World Bank's ideology as regards the infrastructure development with reference to the move of Andhra Pradesh Government to break up the State Electricity Board and Privatise power generation, transmission and distribution, which are bound to raise the cost of power supply and be a major set-back to the development of State. According to Arun Ghosh the APSEB has led the whole country in the matter of efficient power development. Now it is for the Andhra Pradesh, that kow-towing the World Bank ideology in regard to this vital sector would precipitate and economic disaster with "the prospect of the prolonged spell of complete absence of any development, of food shortage, of increasing immiserisation of the people, and civil unrest."[19] He further warned" we have an up-coming scam which will overshadow all previous scams which have bedeviled the country since 1992".[20]

In view of the risks involved in the privatisation of PASEB, the AP Government has to take precautionary steps to safeguard the interests of the State, specially with reference to the electricity tariff to be charged for different purposes. The tariff rates have to facilitate the growth of different sectors of the economy. Attempts at profiteering by charging abnormal rates have to be curbed with appropriate conditionalities and the regulations of the contracts.

The Government of A.P. over the last two years has embarked on a pragmatic policy of democratisation and decentralisation of the administration of the development effort through policies like PVP, Janmabhoomi Development Programmes and formation of water utilisation committee to improve the irrigation system. There is a visible change in the style of Government administration to advance the rural development and development of the State. Hope it will do the needful for avoiding deleterious consequences arising out of the privatisation of APSEB.

The real answer for development to eliminate poverty in developing countries lies in appropriate human resource development to facilitate self-reliant development. In the words of political scientist, Karl Levitt, "Development ultimately is not a matter of GNP of money, or physical capital, or foreign exchange but of the capacity to free up people and empower people to exercise their intelligence and their individual and collective efforts to achieve better life.[21] Hence social development to advance the capabilities of people constitutes a crucial requirement of economic development.

(47) Gunnar Myrdal provocative "Asian Drama: An enquiry into poverty of Nations", rightly pointed that the Asian countries including India have become soft states. The Governments do not have the political will to raise the resources required for accelerating and sustaining economic development. They are just incapable of cutting down on subsidies. They are scared even to be able to think of enforcing discipline upon labour force in the public sector projects to ensure reasonable return on investments.

ECONOMICS OF POWER

Powerful leadership is a great resource for national development. Powerful development leadership builds better democracy. Powerful gentlemen leadership promotes welfare state. But powerful gentlemen are a rare species. Power rulers, power-dealers and power-traders are galore. Hence power corrupts, absolute power corrupts absolutely. The hydra-headed power monster functions in diverse ways among diverse persons. Power makes or mars persons without any relation of their contribution or character. The misuse of power assumes innumerable forms. Power seeking and making kindle social differentiation by caste, religion, region, language, profession, poverty, backwardness and social status. Power facilities and accumulation of wealth and the emergence of parallel economy. Power with diverse persons functions in diverse ways. Democracy may also bristle with tyrants as Mussolini visualised.

Power makes men feudalists, capitalists and fascists. Power kills men of truth, justice, ability and integrity. Power promotes the worshippers of mammon. Power perpetuates wickedness. Power covers up wicked activities. Power multiplies evil activities without limits. Power promotes exploitation of multi-farious ways. Power transforms some men as divine creatures or Gods. Power kindles super egoism. Power promotes intellectual murders. Power devils are great criminals. Powerful leaders detest reason and enlightment. Powerful leaders loose Government due to stupid egoism and unlimited corruption.

According to Benito Mussolini "Democracy is a kingless

regime infested by many kings who are sometimes more exclusive, tyrannical and destructive than one, if he is a tyrant". Tyranny over the virtuous is an abominable crime in any regime.

ECONOMIC IDEAS

The quintessence of D.L. Narayana's economic ideas as expressed in his books, articles, conference papers, speeches and research survey reports postulate him as an advocate of economic and social policy for the early achievement of Welfare State with accelerated economic growth based on proper structural strategies, and requisite emphasis on human resource development, rural development, employment generation, population planning , gender justice, promotion of work ethic and duty mindedness on the part of work force, toning up institutional efficiency in different walks of life, the arresting of declining values with concerted to control rabid social evils such as corruption, casteism, communlism, criminalistion of public life, cold terrorism and destructive class struggle commitment of entrepreneurship, bureaucracy, political parties and Government of social welfare to eradicate sweating, poverty and backwardness, promotion of human spirit of self-reliance, dignity of labour, honesty, integrity, efficiency and sacrifice for a good cause thereby advancing corporate spirit and social discipline to build up favourbale environment for social development and economic development to facilitate vibrant participatory growth.

The erosion of normal values, falling standards of human behaviour and deepening crisis in character are widening the contemporary social crisis spreading social instability. The abysmal deterioration in political culture with least motivation for social service accounts for deepening crisis of values. State and market have to play a cooperative and complementary role in development as in the case of South Asian countries known as Asian Tigers. Financial management of development through the mobilisation of domestic savings, foreign aid, inflow of foreign capital and technology, financial resources and the entrepreneurial support of non-resident Indians as in the case of China where Diaspora played a vital role in the market-oriented economic development. The current social chaos and the evolving social pollution with several corroding evils is more deleterious to growth culture than the environmental pollution for achieving sustained economic development with equity. Effective leadership in different walks of life is the need of the hour for improving social efficiency to achieve take-off in socio economic development to provide better opportunities and quality of life for the increasing millions of India. A person who contributes more than he takes is a donor to socio-economic development. A person who appropriates more than his due to his marginal productivity which is rather difficult to define and specific precisely, is a robber. Those practice regular corruption come under this category. Establishment of this ethical social idealism even at a normal level facilitates righteous and robust development in a perilous parallel economy. Increasing greed for power and riches at the cost of ethical values on the part of vested interests is generating social problems. "No society can surely be flourishing and happy of which by far the greater part of its number are poor and miserable".—(Adam Smith. 1776).

CONCLUSIONS

(1) Free India has acquitted as an Asian tiger in population explosion and parallel economy. As corruption has become a way of life. India has become an expanding mine of scams. Corruption is spreading like a cancer in the Indian economic development entitling the country, for a place among the top ten countries of highest corruption. It is a matter of surmise whether the rate of exploitation in India's parallel economy is greater than the colonial exploitation under the British rule.

(2) Bureaucratic corruption is undermining the impact and efficiency of the programmes of rural development for alleviation of poverty. Right to information through legislation will go a long way to check the corruption by social auditing. If the villagers are well-organised and emerge as control-vailing power, they can exercise decisive impact on the authorities implementing the schemes to derive the benefits of the schemes.

(3) Judicial activism is a prime requisite for awarding

appropriate punishment to the corrupt persons regardless of their political or social status. Appropriate legislative steps are to be taken to bring the culprits under control whether they are MLAs, MPs or such public men or elite bureaucrats.

(4) Firm determination of political parties to eradicate corruption ruthlessly in the country is the top-most requisite, even if they are legislators or public leaders. Dictatorial implementation of measures to check corruption is a necessity, as the politicians with vested interests may sabotage the attempts to control corruption.

(5) As the election expenses constitute the starting point of incurring heavy expenditure, the competitors in election are getting involved in a vicious circle of corruption to mobilise funds and utilise them for getting elected repeatedly. State funding of the parliament and State Legislature elections may obviate the vicious of corruption on the part of the peoples' representatives. The issues needs deeper examination.

(6) It is alarming to note that half a century of loan financing by World Bank rendered poor countries poorer. Development of social capabilities is an essential requisite for advancing the poor countries.

(7) Human Resource Development with knowledge, skills and values is essential to facilitate impressive economic growth. Appointment of right persons with professional excellence, abilities and values as administrators will go a long way to improve the efficient working of universities and provide quality manpower with values to advance healthy social progress and economic development.

(8) Politicisation and rampant corruption account for the deepening crisis of deteriorating values which must be checked by appropriate action when they emerge as social evils.

(9) A paradox of the parallel economy is the very generators of the problem have to be its regulators involving a premium on its successful control.

(10). Persons who thrive on corruption as a regular profession are robbers. Radical public opinion may function as one of the remedies for the menace.

(11) A national movement to wage war against corruption is an imperative need of the country today. It will mean a battle against power-holders, power-dealers and power brokers in different walks of life and the rampant political hypocrisy prevailing in the country.

(12) Other things being equal, it is easier to fight against colonial rule rather than native rule. With increasing transperancy, and consciousness of people and the information revolution, conditions have changed. Although freedom from corruption may mean as much struggle as our freedom struggle, a vibrant popular movement may render the task easier.

The level of corruption prevailing in the country is a stumbling block to the requisite higher economic development. Ultimately it is effective management that creates social and economic development. Efficient management of the economy with appropriate priorities and ethical values facilities equitable development. Government has to muster political will and discard the approach of soft state to tackle the problems.

Notes and References

1. K.M. Panikkar: *A Survey of Indian History*, p. 101.
2. Gunnar Myrdal: *The Challenge of World Poverty, A World Anti-Poverty Programme in Outline*, A Penguin International Edition, 1970, p. 229
3. *Ibid.*, p. 230
4. *Ibid.*
5. *Ibid.*, p. 231
6. K.P. Joseph: "Lessons from Bihar Fodder Scam", *Economic and Political Weekly*, Vol. xxxii. No. 28. July 12-18 1997, p. 1686.
7. Bathuk Gathani: "Corruption is a Global Phenomenon: Says Survey", *The Hindu*, p. 10, *Oct.* 6-10, 1996, Chennai.
8. Dr. John Echeverri-Gent: *The State and the Poor in Public Policy and Political Development in India and United States*, Vikas Publications, New Delhi.
9. Indira Hiraway and Piet Terhal: *Towards Employment Guarantee in India,*

Indo-Dutch Studies on Development Alternatives, Sage Publications, New Delhi, 1994.

10. Anjali Bagwe, "Of Women—The Experience of Rural India". *The Hindu*, March 19, 1996, p. 27, Chennai.
11. Soma Basu: "Unknown Faces and Determined Minds", *The Hindu*, July 27, 1997, p. 2, Chennai.
12. *Ibid.*
13. Bunker Roy: "Where does all the Money Go? Peoples Struggle for Information", *Economic and Political Weekly*, Vol. xxxii, No. 28, July 12-18, 1997, p. 1688.
14. F. Harbison: *Human Resources and Wealth of Nations*, Oxford University Press, 1983, p. 3
15. Mahmood bin Muhammad "Human Values, the Missing Link", *The Hindu*, November 26, 1996, p. 25, Chennai.
16. *Ibid.*
17. Catherine Caufield: "Master of Illusion: The World Bank the Poverty of Nations", Review, " *The Hindu*", August 3, 1997, p. ixv, Chennai.
18. Arun Ghosh: "Break-up and Privatisation of SEB in Andhra Pradesh: An Upcoming Scam", *Economic and Political Weekly*, Vol. xxxii, No. 29, July 19-25, 1997, p. 1782.
19. *Ibid.*, p. 1785.
20. *Ibid.*
21. *The Hindu*, August 3, 1997, p. xiv.

Index